The Poetry of Lewis Carroll

The Poetry of Lewis Carroll

This edition published in 2020 by Arcturus Publishing Limited
26/27 Bickels Yard, 151–153 Bermondsey Street,
London SE1 3HA

AD007501UK

Printed in the UK

Contents

Introduction

Lewis Carroll, born Charles Lutwidge Dodgson in 1832 at Daresbury parsonage in Cheshire, was a brilliant man. He excelled at many things: as a novelist, poet, pamphleteer, mathematician, photographer, artist, inventor, gadgeteer, correspondent, cleric and Oxford don. He was one of 11 children born to the local priest Charles Dodgson and his wife Frances Lutwidge. The family lived in rural seclusion for the first 11 years of their eldest son's life. With little to entertain him, the eccentric boy became the family's circus ringmaster, inventing games, telling stories, writing poems and drawing pictures for a family magazine. He was thought to be a little eccentric by his doting parents, perhaps because he was prone to illness and deaf in one ear. He also developed a stammer at a young age that would remain with him throughout his life.

He left home for school at the age of 12, and while he hated his time at Richmond and Rugby schools, his intellect developed well and he excelled, particularly in maths, a subject in which he received a first-class honours degree from Oxford University in 1854. A year later, he was appointed a lecturer in mathematics at the university, taking up residence in Christ Church where he would remain for much of his life. At the time, Christ Church dons were required to take clerical orders and remain unmarried, conditions to which he adhered, though he did not follow in his father's footsteps by being ordained.

Dodgson continued to write poetry, plays and short stories in which he showed an extraordinary talent for wordplay, 'nonsense' – already made popular by his contemporary Edward Lear – and a unique imagination. Much of his work was published anonymously in newspapers and magazines. However, one editor persuaded him to adopt a pseudonym before publishing 'The Path of Roses' in 1856. Dodgson's invention was ingenious: 'Charles Lutwidge' translated into Latin as 'Carolus Ludovicus', which translated back to English as 'Carroll Lewis' and was then reversed to make 'Lewis Carroll'.

The author's change of name seemed to herald a creative surge. In 1865, he published the book that would make him famous. *Alice's Adventures in Wonderland* was an immediate commercial success, as was its sequel, *Through the Looking-Glass and What Alice Found There* (1871). He also produced poetry collections, which included nonsense poems, narrative verse and more serious works: maths books on Euclid, algebra and the theory of determinants, plus, of course, the most famous nonsense poem in the English language, *The Hunting of the Snark*, published in 1876. These would all feature in a bibliography that numbered more than 300 works by the time he died from pneumonia at his family home in Guildford in 1898.

My Fairy

I have a fairy by my side
  Which says I must not sleep,
When once in pain I loudly cried
  It said 'You must not weep.'

If, full of mirth, I smile and grin,
  It says 'You must not laugh,'
When once I wished to drink some gin,
  It said 'You must not quaff.'

When once a meal I wished to taste
  It said 'You must not bite,'
When to the wars I went in haste,
  It said 'You must not fight.'

'What may I do?' at length I cried,
  Tired of the painful task,
The fairy quietly replied,
  And said 'You must not ask.'

  Moral: 'You mustn't.'

Brother and Sister

'Sister, sister, go to bed,
Go and rest your weary head,'
Thus the prudent brother said.

'Do you want a battered hide
Or scratches to your face applied?'
Thus his sister calm replied.

'Sister! Do not raise my wrath,
I'd make you into mutton broth
As easily as kill a moth.'

The sister raised her beaming eye,
And looked on him indignantly,
And sternly answered 'Only try!'

Off to the cook he quickly ran,
'Dear cook, please lend a frying pan
To me, as quickly as you can.'

'And wherefore should I lend it you?'
'The reason, cook, is plain to view,
I wish to make an Irish stew.'

'What meat is in that stew to go?'
'My sister'll be the contents.' 'Oh!'
'Will you lend the pan, cook?' 'NO!'

Moral: 'Never stew your sister.'

Punctuality

Man naturally loves delay,
    And to procrastinate;
Business put off from day to day
    Is always done too late.

Let every hour be in its place
    Firm fixed, nor loosely shift,
And well enjoy the vacant space,
    As though a birthday gift.

And when the hour arrives, be there,
    Where'er that 'there' may be;
Uncleanly hands or ruffled hair
    Let no one ever see.

If dinner at 'half past' be placed,
    At 'half past' then be dressed,
If at a 'quarter past' make haste
    To be down with the rest.

Better to be before you time,
    Than e'er to be behind;
To open the door while strikes the chime,
    That shows a punctual mind.

Moral:
'Let punctuality and care
    Seize every flitting hour,
So shalt thou cull a floweret fair,
    E'en from a fading flower.'

Rules and Regulations

A short direction
To avoid dejection:
By variations
In occupations,
And prolongation
Of relaxation,
And combinations
Of recreations,
And disputations
On the state of the nation
In adaptation
To your station,
By invitations
To friends and relations,
By evitation
Of amputation,
By permutation
In conversation,
And deep reflection
You'll avoid dejection.

Learn well your grammar,
And never stammer,
Write well and neatly,
And sing most sweetly,
Be enterprising,
Love early rising,
Go walks of six miles,
Have ready quick smiles.
With lightsome laughter,

Soft flowing after.
Drink tea, not coffee;
Never eat toffy.
Eat bread with butter.
Once more, don't stutter.
Don't waste your money,
Abstain from honey.
Shut doors behind you,
(Don't slam them, mind you.)
Drink beer, not porter.
Don't enter the water,
Till to swim you are able.
Sit close to the table.
Take care of a candle.
Shut a door by the handle,
Don't push with your shoulder
Until you are older.
Lose not a button.
Refuse cold mutton,
Starve your canaries,
Believe in fairies.
If you are able,
Don't have a stable
With any mangers.
Be rude to strangers.

Moral: 'Behave.'

Solitude

I love the stillness of the wood,
    I love the music of the rill,
I love to couch in pensive mood
    Upon some silent hill.

Scarce heard, beneath yon arching trees,
    The silver-crested ripples pass;
And, like a mimic brook, the breeze
    Whispers among the grass.

Here from the world I win release,
    Nor scorn of men, nor footstep rude,
Break in to mar the holy peace
    Of this great solitude.

Here may the silent tears I weep
    Lull the vexed spirit into rest,
As infants sob themselves to sleep
    Upon a mother's breast.

But when the bitter hour is gone,
    And the keen throbbing pangs are still,
Oh, sweetest then to couch alone
    Upon some silent hill!

To live in joys that once have been,
    To put the cold world out of sight,
And deck life's drear and barren scene
    With hues of rainbow light.

For what to man the gift of breath,
    If sorrow be his lot below;
If all the day that ends in death
    Be dark with clouds of woe?

Shall the poor transport of an hour
    Repay long years of sore distress –
The fragrance of a lonely flower
    Make glad the wilderness?

Ye golden hours of life's young spring,
    Of innocence, of love and truth!
Bright, beyond all imagining,
    Thou fairy dream of youth!

I'd give all wealth that years have piled,
    The slow result of life's decay,
To be once more a little child
    For one bright summer day.

The Path of Roses

[*Written soon after the Crimean War, when the name of Florence Nightingale had already become a household word, dear to all true British hearts.*]

In the dark silence of an ancient room,
Whose one tall window fronted to the West,
Where, through laced tendrils of a hanging vine,
The sunset glow was fading into night,
Sat a pale Lady, resting weary hands
Upon a great clasped volume, and her face
Within her hands. Not as in rest she bowed,
But large hot tears went coursing down her cheek,
And her low-panted sobs broke awfully
Upon the sleeping echoes of the night.
    Soon she unclasped the volume once again,
And read the words in tone of agony,
As in self-torture, weeping as she read:

'He crowns the glory of his race;
He prayeth but in some fair place
To meet his foeman face to face;

'And battling for the true, the right,
From ruddy dawn to purple night,
To perish in the midmost fight;

'Where foes are fierce and weapons strong,
Where roars the battle loud and long,
Where blood is dropping in the throng.

'Still, with a dim and glazing eye
To watch the tide of victory,
To hear in death the battle-cry.

'Then, gathered grandly to his grave,
To rest among the true and brave,
In holy ground, where yew-trees wave;

'Where, from church-windows sculptured fair,
Float out upon the evening air
The note of praise, the voice of prayer;

'Where no vain marble mockery
Insults with loud and boastful lie
The simple soldier's memory;

'Where sometimes little children go,
And read, in whispered accent slow,
The name of him who sleeps below.'

Her voice died out; like one in dreams she sat.
'Alas!' she sighed, 'for what can woman do?
Her life is aimless, and her death unknown;
Hemmed in by social forms she pines in vain:
Man has his work, but what can woman do?'
        And answer came there from the creeping gloom,
The creeping gloom that settled into night:
'Peace, for thy lot is other than a man's;
His is a path of thorns; he beats them down –
He faces death – he wrestles with despair:
Thine is of roses; to adorn and cheer
His barren lot, and hide the thorns in flowers.'

She spake again, in bitter tone she spake;
'Aye, as a toy, the puppet of an hour;
Or a fair posy, newly plucked at morn,
But flung aside and withered ere the night.'

And answer came there from the creeping gloom,
The creeping gloom that blackened into night:
'So shalt thou be the lamp to light his path,
What time the shades of sorrow close around.'

And, so it seemed to her, an awful light
Pierced slowly through the darkness, orbed, and grew,
Until all passed away – the ancient room –
The sunlight dying through the trellised vine –
The one tall window – all had passed away,
And she was standing on the mighty hills.

Beneath, around, and far as eye could see,
Squadron on squadron, stretched opposing hosts,
Ranked as for battle, mute and motionless.
Anon a distant thunder shook the ground,
The tramp of horses, and a troop shot by –
Plunged headlong in that living sea of men –
Plunged to their death: back from that fatal field
A scattered handful, fighting hard for life,
Broke through the serried lines; but, as she gazed
They shrank and melted, and their forms grew thin –
Grew pale as ghosts when the first morning ray
Dawns from the East – the trumpet's brazen blare
Died into silence – and the vision passed; –

Passed to a room where sick and dying lay,
In long, sad line – there brooded Fear and Pain –
Darkness was there, the shade of Azrael's wing.
But there was one that ever, to and fro,
Moved with light footfall: purely calm her face,

And those deep steadfast eyes that starred the gloom:
Still as she went, she ministered to each
Comfort and counsel; cooled the fevered brow
With softest touch, and in the listening ear
Of the pale sufferer whispered words of peace.
The dying warrior, gazing as she passed,
Clasped his thin hands and blessed her. Bless her too,
Thou who didst bless the merciful of old!

    So prayed the Lady, watching tearfully
Her gentle moving onward, till the night
Had veiled her wholly, and the vision passed.

    Then once again the awful whisper came:
'So in the darkest path of man's despair,
Where War and Terror shake the troubled earth,
Lies woman's mission; with unblenching brow
To pass through scenes of anguish and affright
Where men grow sick and tremble; unto her
All things are sanctified, for all are good.
Nothing so mean, but shall deserve her care;
Nothing so great, but she may bear her part.
No life is vain: each hath his place assigned:
Do thou thy task, and leave the rest to heaven.'
And there was silence, but the Lady made
No answer, save one deeply-breathed 'Amen.'

    And she arose, and in that darkening room
Stood lonely as a spirit of the night –
Stood calm and fearless in the gathered night –
And raised her eyes to heaven. There were tears
Upon her face, but in her heart was peace,
Peace that the world nor gives nor takes away!

Lays of Sorrow

The day was wet, the rain fell souse
     Like jars of strawberry jam, a
Sound was heard in the old hen-house,
     A beating of a hammer.
Of stalwart form, and visage warm,
     Two youths were seen within it,
Splitting up an old tree into perches for their poultry
     At a hundred strokes a minute.

The work is done, the hen has taken
Possession of her nest and eggs,
Without a thought of eggs and bacon,
(Or I am very much mistaken:)
     She turns over each shell,
     To be sure that all's well
     Looks into the straw
     To see there's no flaw,
     Goes once round the house,
     Half afraid of a mouse,
     Then sinks calmly to rest
     On the top of her nest,
First doubling up each of her legs.

Time rolled away, and so did every shell,
     'Small by degrees and beautifully less,'
As the sage mother with a powerful spell
     Forced each in turn its contents to 'express,'
     But ah! 'imperfect is expression,'
     Some poet said, I don't care who,
     If you want to know you must go elsewhere,

One fact I can tell, if you're willing to hear,
He never attended a Parliament Session,
For I'm certain that if he had ever been there,
Full quickly would he have changed his ideas,
With the hissings, the hootings, the groans and
    the cheers.
And as to his name it is pretty clear
That it wasn't me and it wasn't you!

And so it fell upon a day,
    (That is, it never rose again,)
A chick was found upon the hay,
Its little life had ebbed away.
No longer frolicsome and gay,
No longer could it run or play.
'And must we, chicken, must we part?'
Its master cried with bursting heart,
    And voice of agony and pain.
So one, whose ticket's marked 'Return,'
When to the lonely roadside station
He flies in fear and perturbation,
Thinks of his home – the hissing urn –
Then runs with flying hat and hair,
And, entering, finds to his despair
    He's missed the very last train!
Too long it were to tell of each conjecture
    Of chicken suicide, and poultry victim,
The deadly frown, the stern and dreary lecture,
    The timid guess, 'perhaps some needle pricked him!'
The din of voice, the words both loud and many,
    The sob, the tear, the sigh that none could smother,
Till all agreed: 'a shilling to a penny

It killed itself, and we acquit the mother!'
Scarce was the verdict spoken,
When that still calm was broken,
A childish form hath burst into the throng;
With tears and looks of sadness,
That bring no news of gladness,
But tell too surely something hath gone wrong!
'The sight I have come upon
The stoutest heart would sicken,
That nasty hen has been and gone
And killed another chicken!'

Red Riding-Hood

Into the wood – the dark, dark wood –
    Forth went the happy Child;
And, in its stillest solitude,
    Talked to herself, and smiled:
And closer drew the scarlet Hood
    About her ringlets wild.

And now at last she threads the maze,
    And now she need not fear;
Frowning, she meets the sudden blaze
    Of moonlight falling clear;
Nor trembles she, nor turns, nor stays,
    Although the Wolf be near.

Photography Extraordinary

The Milk-and-Water School
Alas! she would not hear my prayer!
Yet it were rash to tear my hair;
Disfigured, I should be less fair.

She was unwise, I may say blind;
Once she was lovingly inclined;
Some circumstance has changed her mind.

The Strong-Minded or Matter-of-Fact School
Well! so my offer was no go!
She might do worse, I told her so;
She was a fool to answer 'No.'

However, things are as they stood;
Nor would I have her if I could,
For there are plenty more as good.

The Spasmodic or German School
Firebrands and daggers! hope hath fled!
To atoms dash the doubly dead!
My brain is fire – my heart is lead!

Her soul is flint, and what am I?
Scorch'd by her fierce, relentless eye,
Nothingness is my destiny!

The Palace of Humbug

I dreamt I dwelt in marble halls,
And each damp thing that creeps and crawls
Went wobble-wobble on the walls.

Faint odours of departed cheese,
Blown on the dank, unwholesome breeze,
Awoke the never-ending sneeze.

Strange pictures decked the arras drear,
Strange characters of woe and fear,
The humbugs of the social sphere.

One showed a vain and noisy prig,
That shouted empty words and big
At him that nodded in a wig.

And one, a dotard grim and grey,
Who wasteth childhood's happy day
In work more profitless than play.

Whose icy breast no pity warms,
Whose little victims sit in swarms,
And slowly sob on lower forms.

And one, a green thyme-honoured Bank,
Where flowers are growing wild and rank,
Like weeds that fringe a poisoned tank.

All birds of evil omen there
Flood with rich Notes the tainted air,
The witless wanderer to snare.

The fatal Notes neglected fall,
No creature heeds the treacherous call,
For all those goodly Strawn Baits Pall.

The wandering phantom broke and fled,
Straightway I saw within my head
A vision of a ghostly bed,

Where lay two worn decrepit men,
The fictions of a lawyer's pen,
Who never more might breathe again.

The serving man of Richard Roe
Wept, inarticulate with woe:
She wept, that waiting on John Doe.

'Oh rouse', I urged, 'the waning sense
With tales of tangled evidence,
Of suit, demurrer, and defence.'

'Vain', she replied, 'such mockeries:
For morbid fancies, such as these,
No suits can suit, no plea can please.'

And bending o'er that man of straw,
She cried in grief and sudden awe,
Not inappropriately, 'Law!'

The well-remembered voice he knew,
He smiled, he faintly muttered 'Sue!'
(Her very name was legal too.)

The night was fled, the dawn was nigh:
A hurricane went raving by,
And swept the Vision from mine eye.

Vanished that dim and ghostly bed,
(The hangings, tape; the tape was red:)
'Tis o'er, and Doe and Roe are dead!

Oh, yet my spirit inly crawls,
What time it shudderingly recalls
That horrid dream of marble halls!

Upon the Lonely Moor

I met an aged, aged man
    Upon the lonely moor:
I knew I was a gentleman,
    And he was but a boor.
So I stopped and roughly questioned him,
    'Come, tell me how you live!'
But his words impressed my ear no more
    Than if it were a sieve.

He said, 'I look for soap-bubbles,
    That lie among the wheat,
And bake them into mutton-pies,
    And sell them in the street.
I sell them unto men', he said,
    'Who sail on stormy seas;
And that's the way I get my bread –
    A trifle, if you please.'

But I was thinking of a way
    To multiply by ten,
And always, in the answer, get
    The question back again.
I did not hear a word he said,
    But kicked that old man calm,
And said, 'Come, tell me how you live!'
    And pinched him in the arm.

His accents mild took up the tale:
    He said, 'I go my ways,
And when I find a mountain-rill,

I set it in a blaze.
And thence they make a stuff they call
　　Rowland's Macassar Oil;
But fourpence-halfpenny is all
　　They give me for my toil.'

But I was thinking of a plan
　　To paint one's gaiters green,
So much the colour of the grass
　　That they could ne'er be seen.
I gave his ear a sudden box,
　　And questioned him again,
And tweaked his grey and reverend locks,
　　And put him into pain.

He said, 'I hunt for haddocks' eyes
　　Among the heather bright,
And work them into waistcoat-buttons
　　In the silent night.
And these I do not sell for gold,
　　Or coin of silver-mine,
But for a copper-halfpenny,
　　And that will purchase nine.

'I sometimes dig for buttered rolls,
　　Or set limed twigs for crabs;
I sometimes search the flowery knolls
　　For wheels of hansom cabs.
And that's the way' (he gave a wink)
　　'I get my living here,
And very gladly will I drink
　　Your Honour's health in beer.'

I heard him then, for I had just
    Completed my design
To keep the Menai bridge from rust
    By boiling it in wine.
I duly thanked him, ere I went,
    For all his stories queer,
But chiefly for his kind intent
    To drink my health in beer.

And now if e'er by chance I put
    My fingers into glue,
Or madly squeeze a right-hand foot
    Into a left-hand shoe;
Or if a statement I aver
    Of which I am not sure,
I think of that strange wanderer
    Upon the lonely moor.

Acrostic

Little maidens, when you look
On this little story-book,
Reading with attentive eye
Its enticing history;
Never think that hours of play
Are your only holiday,
And that, in a time of joy
Lessons serve but to annoy.
If in any HOUSE you find
Children of a gentle mind,
Each the others pleasing ever,
Each the others vexing never,
Daily work and pastime daily
In their order taking gaily –
Then be very sure that they
Have a life of HOLIDAY.

Stolen Waters

The light was faint, and soft the air
    That breathed around the place;
And she was lithe, and tall, and fair,
    And with a wayward grace
    Her queenly head she bare.

With glowing cheek, with gleaming eye,
    She met me on the way:
My spirit owned the witchery
    Within her smile that lay:
I followed her, I knew not why.

The trees were thick with many a fruit,
    The grass with many a flower:
My soul was dead, my tongue was mute,
    In that accursëd hour.

And, in my dream, with silvery voice,
    She said, or seemed to say,
'Youth is the season to rejoice –'
    I could not choose but stay;
    I could not say her nay.

She plucked a branch above her head,
    With rarest fruitage laden:
'Drink of the juice, Sir Knight,' she said,
    ''Tis good for knight and maiden.'

Oh, blind mine eye that would not trace –
    And deaf mine ear that would not heed –

The mocking smile upon her face,
 The mocking voice of greed!

I drank the juice, and straightway felt
 A fire within my brain;
My soul within me seemed to melt
 In sweet delirious pain.

'Sweet is the stolen draught,' she said;
 'Hath sweetness stint or measure?
Pleasant the secret hoard of bread;
 What bars us from our pleasure?'

'Yea, take we pleasure while we may,'
 I heard myself replying;
In the red sunset, far away,
 My happier life was dying:
My heart was sad, my voice was gay.

And unawares, I knew not how,
 I kissed her dainty finger-tips,
I kissed her on the lily brow,
 I kissed her on the false, false lips –
That burning kiss, I feel it now!

'True love gives true love of the best:
 Then take,' I cried, 'my heart to thee!'
The very heart from out my breast
 I plucked, I gave it willingly:
 Her very heart she gave to me –
Then died the glory from the west.

In the grey light I saw her face,
      And it was withered, old, and grey;
The flowers were fading in their place,
      Were fading with the fading day.

Forth from her, like a hunted deer,
      Through all that ghastly night I fled,
And still behind me seemed to hear
      Her fierce unflagging tread;
And scarce drew breath for fear.

Yet marked I well how strangely seemed
      The heart within my breast to sleep:
Silent it lay, or so I dreamed,
      With never a throb nor leap.

For hers was now my heart, she said,
      The heart that once had been mine own:
And in my breast I bore instead
      A cold, cold heart of stone.
So grew the morning overhead.

The sun shot downward through the trees
      His old familiar flame;
All ancient sounds upon the breeze
      From copse and meadow came –
      But I was not the same.

They call me mad; I smile, I weep,
      Uncaring how or why:
Yea, when one's heart is laid asleep,

What better than to die?
So that the grave be dark and deep.

To die! To die? And yet, methinks,
    I drink of life to-day,
Deep as the thirsty traveller drinks
    Of fountain by the way:
    My voice is sad, my heart is gay.

When yestereve was on the wane,
    I heard a clear voice singing;
And suddenly, like summer-rain,
    My happy tears came springing:
My human heart returned again.

    'A rosy child –
Sitting and singing, in a garden fair,
    The joy of hearing, seeing,
    The simple joy of being –
Or twining rosebuds in the golden hair
    That ripples free and wild.

    'A sweet pale child –
Wearily looking to the purple West –
    Waiting the great For-ever
    That suddenly shall sever
The cruel chains that hold her from her rest –
    By earth-joys unbeguiled.

    'An angel-child –
Gazing with living eyes on a dead face:

The mortal form forsaken,
That none may now awaken,
That lieth painless, moveless in her place,
As though in death she smiled!

'Be as a child —
So shalt thou sing for very joy of breath —
So shalt thou wait thy dying,
In holy transport lying —
So pass rejoicing through the gate of death,
In garment undefiled.'

Then call me what they will, I know
That now my soul is glad:
If this be madness, better so,
Far better to be mad,
Weeping or smiling as I go.

For if I weep, it is that now
I see how deep a loss is mine,
And feel how brightly round my brow
The coronal might shine,
Had I but kept mine early vow:

And if I smile, it is that now
I see the promise of the years —
The garland waiting for my brow,
That must be won with tears,
With pain — with death — I care not how.

The Crocodile

How doth the little crocodile
    Improve his shining tail,
And pour the waters of the Nile
    On every golden scale!

How cheerfully he seems to grin,
    How neatly spreads his claws,
And welcomes little fishes in,
    With gently smiling jaws!

The Elections to the Hebdomadal Council

[In the year 1866, a Letter with the above title was published in Oxford, addressed by Mr Goldwin Smith to the Senior Censor of Christ Church, with the twofold object of revealing to the University a vast political misfortune which it had unwittingly encountered, and of suggesting a remedy which should at once alleviate the bitterness of the calamity and secure the sufferers from its recurrence. The misfortune thus revealed was no less than the fact that, at a recent election of Members to the Hebdomadal Council, two Conservatives had been chosen, thus giving a Conservative majority in the Council; and the remedy suggested was a sufficiently sweeping one, embracing, as it did, the following details: –

1. 'The exclusion' (from Congregation) 'of the non-academical elements which form a main part of the strength of this party domination.' These 'elements' are afterwards enumerated as 'the parish clergy and the professional men of the city, and chaplains who are without any academical occupation.'

2. The abolition of the Hebdomadal Council.

3. The abolition of the legislative functions of Convocation.

These are all the main features of this remarkable scheme of Reform, unless it be necessary to add –

4. 'To preside over a Congregation with full legislative powers, the Vice-Chancellor ought no doubt to be a man of real capacity.'

But it would be invidious to suppose that there was any intention of suggesting this as a novelty.

The following rhythmical version of the Letter develops its principles to an extent which possibly the writer had never contemplated.]

'Now is the *Winter* of our discontent.'[1]

'Heard ye the arrow hurtle in the sky?
Heard ye the dragon-monster's deathful cry?' –
Excuse this sudden burst of the Heroic;
The present state of things would vex a Stoic!
And just as Sairey Gamp, for pains within,
Administered a modicum of gin,
So does my mind, when vexed and ill at ease,
Console itself with soothing similes.
The 'dragon-monster' (pestilential schism!)
I need not tell you is Conservatism;
The 'hurtling arrow' (till we find a better)
Is represented by the present Letter.
        'Twas, I remember, but the other day,
Dear Senior Censor, that you chanced to say
You thought these party-combinations would
Be found, 'though needful, no unmingled good.'
Unmingled good? They are unmingled ill![2]
I never took to them, and never will[3] –
What am I saying? Heed it not, my friend:
On the next page I mean to recommend
The very dodges that I now condemn
In the Conservatives! Don't hint to them }
A word of this! (In confidence. Ahem!) }
Need I rehearse the history of Jowett?
I need not, Senior Censor, for you know it.[4]
That was the Board Hebdomadal, and oh!
Who would be free, themselves must strike the blow!

Let each that wears a beard, and each that shaves,
Join in the cry 'We never will be slaves!'
'But can the University afford
To be a slave to any kind of board?
A *slave?*' you shuddering ask. 'Think you it can, Sir?'
'*Not at the present moment,*' is my answer.[5]
I've thought the matter o'er and o'er again,
And given to it all my powers of brain;
I've thought it out, and this is what I make it,
(And I don't care a Tory how you take it:)
It may be right to go ahead, I guess:
It may be right to stop, I do confess:
Also, it may be right to retrogress.[6]
So says the oracle, and, for myself, I
Must say it beats to fits the one at Delphi!

    To save beloved Oxford from the yoke,
(For this majority's beyond a joke,)
We must combine,[7] aye! hold a *caucus*-meeting,[8]
Unless we want to get another beating.
That they should 'bottle' us is nothing new –
But shall they bottle us and *caucus* too?
See the 'fell unity of purpose' now
With which Obstructives plunge into the row![9]
'Factious Minorities,' we used to sigh –
'Factious Majorities!' is now the cry.
'Votes – ninety-two' – no combination here:
'Votes – ninety-three' – conspiracy, 'tis clear![10]
You urge "'Tis but a unit." I reply
That in that unit lurks their 'unity.'
Our voters often bolt, and often baulk us,
But then, they never, never go to *caucus*!
Our voters can't forget the maxim famous

'*Semel electum semper eligamus;*'
They never can be worked into a ferment
By visionary promise of preferment,
Nor taught, by hints of 'Paradise'[11] beguiled,
To whisper 'C for Chairman' like a child![12]
And thus the friends that we have tempted down
Oft take the two-o'clock Express for town.[13]

    This is our danger: this the secret foe
That aims at Oxford such a deadly blow.
What champion can we find to save the State,
To crush the plot? We darkly whisper 'Wait!'[14]

    My scheme is this: remove the votes of all
The residents that are not Liberal[15] –
Leave the young Tutors uncontrolled and free,
And Oxford then shall see – what it shall see.
What next? Why then, I say, let Convocation
Be shorn of all her powers of legislation.[16]
But why stop there? Let us go boldly on –
Sweep everything beginning with a 'Con'
Into oblivion! Convocation first,
Conservatism next, and, last and worst,
'*Concilium Hebdomadale*' must,
Consumed and conquered, be consigned to dust![17]

    And here I must relate a little fable
I heard last Saturday at our high table: –
The cats, it seems, were masters of the house,
And held their own against the rat and mouse:
Of course the others couldn't stand it long,
So held a *caucus*, (not, in their case, wrong:)
And, when they were assembled to a man,
Uprose an aged rat, and thus began: –

    'Brothers in bondage! Shall we bear to be

For ever left in a minority?
With what "fell unity of purpose" cats
Oppress the trusting innocence of rats!
So unsuspicious are we of disguise,
Their machinations take us by surprise[18] –
Insulting and tyrannical absurdities![19]
It is too bad by half – upon my word it is!
For, now that these Con——, cats, I should say,
   (frizzle 'em!),
Are masters, they exterminate like Islam![20]
How shall we deal with them? I'll tell you how: –
Let none but kittens be allowed to miaow!
The Liberal kittens seize us but in play,
And, while they frolic, we can run away:
But older cats are not so generous,
Their claws are too Conservative for us!
Then let them keep the stable and the oats,
While kittens, rats, and mice have all the votes.

     'Yes; banish cats! The kittens would not use
Their powers for blind obstruction,[21] nor refuse
To let us sip the cream and gnaw the cheese –
How glorious then would be our destinies![22]
Kittens and rats would occupy the throne,
And rule the larder for itself alone!'[23]

       So rhymed my friend, and asked me what I thought
        of it.
I told him that so much as I had caught of it
Appeared to me (as I need hardly mention)
Entirely undeserving of attention.
But now, to guide the Congregation, when
It numbers none but really 'able' men,
A 'Vice-Cancellarius' will be needed

Of every kind of human weakness weeded!
Is such the president that we have got?
He ought no doubt to be; why should he not?[24]

    I do not hint that Liberals should dare
To oust the present holder of the chair –
But surely he would not object to be
Gently examined by a Board of three?
Their duty being just to ascertain
That he's 'all there' (I mean, of course, in brain),
And that his mind, from 'petty details' clear,
Is fitted for the duties of his sphere.

    All this is merely moonshine, till we get
The seal of Parliament upon it set.
A word then, Senior Censor, in your ear:
The Government is in a state of fear –
Like some old gentleman, abroad at night,
Seized with a sudden shiver of affright,
Who offers money, on his bended knees,
To the first skulking vagabond he sees –
Now is the lucky moment for our task;
They daren't refuse us anything we ask![25]

    And then our Fellowships shall open be
To Intellect, no meaner quality!
No moral excellence, no social fitness
Shall ever be admissible as witness.
'Avaunt, dull Virtue!' is Oxonia's cry:
'Come to my arms, ingenious Villainy!'

    For Classic Fellowships, an honour high,
Simonides and Co. will then apply –
Our Mathematics will to Oxford bring
The 'cutest members of the betting-ring –
Law Fellowships will start upon their journeys

A myriad of unscrupulous attorneys –
While poisoners, doomed till now to toil unknown,
Shall mount the Physical Professor's throne!

    To what a varied feast of learning then
Should we invite our intellectual men!
Professor Caseley should instruct our flock
To analyse the mysteries of Locke –
Barnum should lecture them on Rhetoric –
The Davenports upon the cupboard-trick –
Robson and Redpath, Strahan and Paul and Bates
Should store the minds of undergraduates –
From Fagin's lecture-room a class should come
Versed in all arts of finger and of thumb,
To illustrate in practice (though by stealth)
The transitory character of wealth.
And thus would Oxford educate, indeed,
Men far beyond a merely local need –
With no career before them, I may say, [26]
Unless they're wise enough to go away,
And seek, far West, or in the distant East,
Another flock of pigeons to be fleeced.

    I might go on, and trace the destiny
Of Oxford in an age which, though it be
Thus breaking with tradition, owns a new
Allegiance to the intellectual few –
(I mean, of course, the – pshaw! no matter who!)
But, were I to pursue the boundless theme,
I fear that I should seem to you to dream.[27]
This to fulfil, or even – humbler far –
To shun Conservatism's noxious star
And all the evils that it brings behind,
These pestilential coils must be untwined –   ⎱
These party-coils, that clog the march of Mind – ⎰

Choked in whose meshes Oxford, slowly wise,
Has lain for three disastrous centuries.[28]
Away with them! (It is for this I yearn.)
Each twist untwist, each Turner overturn!
Disfranchise each Conservative, and cancel
The votes of Michell, Liddon, Wall, and Mansel!
Then, then shall Oxford be herself again,
Neglect the heart, and cultivate the brain –
Then this shall be the burden of our song,
'All change is good – whatever is, is wrong' –
Then Intellect's proud flag shall be unfurled,
And Brain, and Brain alone, shall rule the world!

Notes

1. Dr Wynter, President of St. John's, one of the recently elected Conservative members of Council.
2. 'In a letter on a point connected with the late elections to the Hebdomadal Council you incidentally remarked to me that our combinations for these elections, "though necessary, were not an unmixed good." They are an unmixed evil.'
3. 'I never go to a *caucus* without reluctance: I never write a canvassing letter without a feeling of repugnance to my task.'
4. 'I need not rehearse the history of the Regius Professor of Greek.'
5. 'The University cannot afford at the present moment to be delivered over as a slave to any non-academical interest whatever.'
6. 'It may be right to go on, it may be right to stand still, or it may be right to go back.'
7. 'To save the University from going completely under the yoke… we shall still be obliged to combine.'
8. 'Caucus-holding and wire-pulling would still be almost inevitably carried on to some extent.'
9. 'But what are we to do? Here is a great political and theological

party… labouring under perfect discipline and with fell unity of purpose, to hold the University in subjection, and fill her government with its nominees.'

10. At a recent election to Council, the Liberals mustered ninety-two votes, and the Conservatives ninety-three; whereupon the latter were charged with having obtained their victory by a conspiracy.

11. 'Not to mention that, as we cannot promise Paradise to our supporters, they are very apt to take the train for London just before the election.'

12. It is not known to what the word 'Paradise' was intended to allude, and therefore the hint, here thrown out, that the writer meant to recall the case of the late Chairman of Mr Gathorne Hardy's committee, who had been recently collated to the See of Chester, is wholly wanton and gratuitous.

13. A case of this had actually occurred on the occasion of the division just alluded to.

14. Mr Wayte, now President of Trinity, then put forward as the Liberal candidate for election to Council.

15. 'You and others suggest, as the only effective remedy, that the Constituency should be reformed, by the exclusion of the non-academical elements which form a main part of the strength of this party domination.'

16. 'I confess that, having included all the really academical elements in Congregation, I would go boldly on, and put an end to the legislative functions of Convocation.'

17. 'This conviction, that while we have Elections to Council we shall not entirely get rid of party organisation and its evils, leads me to venture a step further, and to raise the question whether it is really necessary that we should have an Elective Council for legislative purposes at all.'

18. Sometimes, indeed, not being informed that the wires are at work, we are completely taken by surprise.'

19. 'We are without protection against this most insulting and tyrannical absurdity.'

20. 'It is as exterminating as Islam.'

21. 'Their powers would scarcely be exercised for the purposes of fanaticism, or in a spirit of blind obstruction.'

22. 'These narrow local bounds, within which our thoughts and schemes

have hitherto been pent, will begin to disappear, and a far wider sphere of action will open on the view.'

23. 'Those councils must be freely opened to all who can serve her well and who will serve her for herself.'

24. 'To preside over a Congregation with full legislative powers, the Vice-Chancellor ought no doubt to be a man of real capacity; but why should he not? His mind ought also, for this as well as for his other high functions, to be clear of petty details, and devoted to the great matters of University business; but why should not this condition also be fulfilled?'

25. 'If you apply now to Parliament for this or any other University reform, you will find the House of Commons in a propitious mood... Even the Conservative Government, as it looks for the support of moderate Liberals on the one great subject, is very unwilling to present itself in such an aspect that these men may not be able decently to give it their support.'

26. 'With open Fellowships, Oxford will soon produce a supply of men fit for the work of high education far beyond her own local demands, and in fact with no career before them unless a career can be opened elsewhere.'

27. 'I should seem to you to dream if I were to say what I think the destiny of the University may be in an age which, though it is breaking with tradition, is, from the same causes, owning a new allegiance to intellectual authority.'

28. 'But to fulfil this, or even a far humbler destiny – to escape the opposite lot – the pestilential coils of party, in which the University has lain for three disastrous centuries choked, must be untwined.'

Hiawatha's Photographing

[In these days of imitation, I can claim no sort of merit for this slight attempt at doing what is known to be so easy. Any one who knows what verse is, with the slightest ear for rhythm, can throw off a composition in the easy running metre of 'The Song of Hiawatha'. Having, then, distinctly stated that I challenge no attention, in the following little poem, to its merely verbal jingle, I must beg the candid reader, to confine his criticism, to its treatment of the subject.]

From his shoulder Hiawatha
Took the camera of rosewood,
Made of sliding, folding rosewood;
Neatly put it all together.
In its case it lay compactly,
Folded into nearly nothing;
But he opened out the hinges,
Pushed and pulled the joints and hinges,
Till it looked all squares and oblongs,
Like a complicated figure
In the Second Book of Euclid.
    This he perched upon a tripod,
And the family in order
Sat before him for their pictures.
Mystic, awful was the process.
    First, a piece of glass he coated
With Collodion, and plunged it
In a bath of Lunar Caustic
Carefully dissolved in water:
There he left it certain minutes.
    Secondly, my Hiawatha
Made with cunning hand a mixture

Of the acid Pyro-gallic,
And of Glacial Acetic,
And of Alcohol and water:
This developed all the picture.

Finally, he fixed each picture
With a saturate solution
Of a certain salt of Soda –
Chemists call it Hyposulphite.
(Very difficult the name is
For a metre like the present
But periphrasis has done it.)

All the family in order
Sat before him for their pictures:
Each in turn, as he was taken,
Volunteered his own suggestions,
His invaluable suggestions.

First the Governor, the Father:
He suggested velvet curtains
Looped about a massy pillar;
And the corner of a table,
Of a rosewood dining-table.
He would hold a scroll of something,
Hold it firmly in his left-hand;
He would keep his right-hand buried
(Like Napoleon) in his waistcoat;
He would contemplate the distance
With a look of pensive meaning,
As of ducks that die in tempests.
He would gaze into the distance –

Grand, heroic was the notion:
Yet the picture failed entirely:
Failed because he moved a little,

Moved because he couldn't help it.

    Next, his better half took courage;
She would have her picture taken;
She came dressed beyond description,
Dressed in jewels and in satin,
Far too gorgeous for an empress.
Gracefully she sat down sideways,
With a simper scarcely human,
Holding in her hand a nosegay
Rather larger than a cabbage.
All the while that she was taking,
Still the lady chattered, chattered,
Like a monkey in the forest.
'Am I sitting still?' she asked him.
'Is my face enough in profile?
Shall I hold the nosegay higher?
Will it come into the picture?'
And the picture failed completely.

    Next the son, the Stunning-Cantab:
He suggested curves of beauty,
Curves pervading all his figure,
Which the eye might follow onward,
Till they centred in the breast-pin,
Centred in the golden breast-pin.
He had learnt it all from Ruskin
(Author of 'The Stones of Venice,'
'Seven Lamps of Architecture,'
'Modern Painters,' and some others);
And perhaps he had not fully
Understood his author's meaning;
But, whatever was the reason,
All was fruitless, as the picture

Ended in an utter failure.

Next to him the eldest daughter:
She suggested very little;
Only asked if he would take her
With her look of 'passive beauty.'

Her idea of passive beauty
Was a squinting of the left-eye,
Was a drooping of the right-eye,
Was a smile that went up sideways
To the corner of the nostrils.

Hiawatha, when she asked him,
Took no notice of the question,
Looked as if he hadn't heard it;
But, when pointedly appealed to,
Smiled in his peculiar manner,
Coughed, and said it 'didn't matter,'
Bit his lip and changed the subject.

Nor in this was he mistaken,
As the picture failed completely.

So, in turn, the other sisters.
Last, the youngest son was taken:
Very rough and thick his hair was,
Very dusty was his jacket,
Very fidgety his manner,
And his overbearing sisters
Called him names he disapproved of:
Called him Johnny, 'Daddy's Darling,'
Called him Jacky, 'Scrubby School-boy.'
And, so awful was the picture,
In comparison the others
Might be thought to have succeeded,
To have partially succeeded.

Finally my Hiawatha
Tumbled all the tribe together,
('Grouped' is not the right expression),
And, as happy chance would have it,
Did at last obtain a picture
Where the faces all succeeded:
Each came out a perfect likeness.

Then they joined and all abused it,
Unrestrainedly abused it,
As 'the worst and ugliest picture
They could possibly have dreamed of.
Giving one such strange expressions —
Sulkiness, conceit, and meanness!
Really any one would take us
(Any one that did not know us)
For the most unpleasant people!'
(Hiawatha seemed to think so,
Seemed to think it not unlikely).
All together rang their voices,
Angry, loud, discordant voices,
As of dogs that howl in concert,
As of cats that wail in chorus.

But my Hiawatha's patience,
His politeness and his patience,
Unaccountably had vanished,
And he left that happy party.
Neither did he leave them slowly,
With the calm deliberation,
The intense deliberation
Which photographers aspire to:
But he left them in a hurry,
Left them in a mighty hurry,

Vowing that he would not stand it.

   Hurriedly he packed his boxes,
Hurriedly the porter trundled
On a barrow all his boxes,
Hurriedly he took his ticket,
Hurriedly the train received him:
Thus departed Hiawatha.

The Lang Coortin'

The ladye she stood at her lattice high,
    Wi' her doggie at her feet;
Thorough the lattice she can spy
    The passers in the street.

'There's one that standeth at the door,
    And tirleth at the pin:
Now speak and say, my popinjay,
    If I sall let him in.'

Then up and spake the popinjay
    That flew abune her head:
'Gae let him in that tirls the pin,
    He cometh thee to wed.'

O when he cam' the parlour in,
    A woeful man was he!
'And dinna ye ken your lover again,
    Sae well that loveth thee?'

'And how wad I ken ye loved me, Sir,
    That have been sae lang away?
And how wad I ken ye loved me, Sir?
    Ye never telled me sae!'

Said – 'ladye dear,' and the salt salt tear
    Cam' rinnin' doon his cheek,
'I have sent thee tokens of my love
    This many and many a week.

'O didna ye get the rings, ladye,
        The rings o' the gowd sae fine?
I wist that I have sent to thee
        Four score, four score and nine.'

'They cam' to me,' said that fair ladye,
        'Wow, they were flimsie things!'
Said – 'that chain o' gowd, my doggie to houd,
        It is made o' thae self-same rings.'

'And didna ye get the locks, the locks,
        The locks o' my ain black hair,
Whilk I sent by post, whilk I sent by box,
        Whilk I sent by the carrier?'

'They cam' to me,' said that fair ladye;
        'And I prithee send nae mair!'
Said – 'that cushion sae red, for my doggie's head,
        It is stuffed wi' thae locks o' hair.'

'And didna ye get the letter, ladye,
        Tied wi' a silken string,
Whilk I sent to thee frae the far countrie,
        A message of love to bring?'

'It cam' to me frae the far countrie
        Wi' its silken string and a';
But it wasna prepaid,' said that high-born maid,
        'Sae I gar'd them tak' it awa'.'

'O ever alack that ye sent it back,
        It was written sae clerkly and well!

Now the message it brought, and the boon that it sought,
    I must even say it mysel'.'

Then up and spake the popinjay,
    Sae wisely counselled he:
'Now say it in the proper way,
    Gae doon upon thy knee!'

The lover he turned baith red and pale,
    Gaed doon upon his knee:
'O ladye, hear the waesome tale
    I have to tell to thee!

'For five lang years, and five lang years,
    I coorted thee by looks;
By nods and winks, by smiles and tears,
    As I had read in books.

'For ten lang years, O weary hours!
    I coorted thee by signs;
By sending game, by sending flowers,
    By sending Valentines.

'For five lang years, and five lang years,
    I have dwelt in the far countrie,
Till that thy mind should be inclined
    Mair tenderly to me.

'Now thirty years are gane and past,
    I am come frae a foreign land:
I am come to tell thee my love at last;
    O Ladye, gie me thy hand!'

The ladye she turned not pale nor red,
        But she smiled a pitiful smile:
'Sic' a coortin' as yours, my man,' she said,
        'Takes a lang and a weary while!'

And out and laughed the popinjay,
        A laugh of bitter scorn:
'A coortin' done in sic' a way,
        It ought not to be borne!'

Wi' that the doggie barked aloud,
        And up and doon he ran,
And tugged and strained his chain o' gowd,
        All for to bite the man.

'O hush thee, gentle popinjay!
        O hush thee, doggie dear!
There is a thing I fain wad say,
        It needeth he should hear!'

Aye louder screamed that ladye fair
        To still her doggie's bark;
Ever the lover shouted mair
        To make that ladye hark:

Shrill and more shrill the popinjay
        Kept up his angry squall:
I trow the doggie's voice that day
        Was louder than them all!

The serving-men and serving-maids
        Sat by the kitchen fire:

They heard sic' a din the parlour within
    As made them much admire.

Out spake the boy in buttons,
    (I ween he wasna thin,)
'Now wha will tae the parlour gae,
    And stay this deadlie din?'

And they have taen a kerchief,
    Casted their kevils in,
For wha should tae the parlour gae,
    And stay that deadlie din.

When on that boy the kevil fell
    To stay the fearsome noise,
'Gae in,' they cried, 'whate'er betide,
    Thou prince of button-boys!'

Syne, he has taen a supple cane
    To beat that dog sae fat:
The doggie yowled, the doggie howled
    The louder aye for that.

Syne, he has taen a mutton-bane –
    The doggie hushed his noise,
And followed doon the kitchen stair
    That prince of button-boys!

Then sadly spake that ladye fair,
    Wi' a frown upon her brow:
'O dearer to me is my sma' doggie
    Than a dozen sic' as thou!

'Nae use, nae use for sighs and tears:
  Nae use at all to fret:
Sin' ye've bided sae well for thirty years,
  Ye may bide a wee langer yet!'

Sadly, sadly he crossed the floor,
  And tirlèd at the pin:
Sadly went he through the door
  Where sadly he cam' in.

'O gin I had a popinjay,
  To fly abune my head,
To tell me what I ought to say,
  I had by now been wed.

'O gin I find anither ladye,'
  He said with sighs and tears,
'I wist my coortin' sall not be
  Anither thirty years.

'For gin I find a ladye gay,
  Exactly to my taste,
I'll pop the question, aye or nay,
  In twenty years at maist.'

Melancholetta

With saddest music all day long
 She soothed her secret sorrow:
At night she sighed 'I fear 'twas wrong
 Such cheerful words to borrow;
Dearest, a sweeter, sadder song
 I'll sing to thee to-morrow.'

I thanked her, but I could not say
 That I was glad to hear it:
I left the house at break of day,
 And did not venture near it
Till time, I hoped, had worn away
 Her grief, for nought could cheer it!

My dismal sister! Couldst thou know
 The wretched home thou keepest!
Thy brother, drowned in daily woe,
 Is thankful when thou sleepest;
For if I laugh, however low,
 When thou'rt awake, thou weepest!

I took my sister t'other day
 (Excuse the slang expression)
To Sadler's Wells to see the play,
 In hopes the new impression
Might in her thoughts, from grave to gay,
 Effect some slight digression.

I asked three gay young dogs from town
 To join us in our folly,

Whose mirth, I thought, might serve to drown
　　My sister's melancholy:
The lively Jones, the sportive Brown,
　　And Robinson the jolly.

I need not tell of soup and fish
　　In solemn silence swallowed,
The sobs that ushered in each dish,
　　And its departure followed,
Nor yet my suicidal wish
　　To *be* the cheese I hollowed.

Some desperate attempts were made
　　To start a conversation;
'Madam,' the lively Jones essayed,
　　'Which kind of recreation,
Hunting or fishing, have you made
　　Your special occupation?'

Her lips curved downwards instantly,
　　As if of india-rubber.
'Hounds *in full cry* I like,' said she:
　　(Oh how I longed to snub her!)
'Of fish, a whale's the one for me,
　　it is so full of blubber!'

The night's performance was 'King John:'
　　'It's dull,' she wept, 'and so-so!'
Awhile I let her tears flow on,
　　She said 'they soothed her woe so!'
At length the curtain rose upon
　　'Bombastes Furioso.'

In vain we roared; in vain we tried
    To rouse her into laughter:
Her pensive glances wandered wide
    From orchestra to rafter –
'Tier upon tier!' she said, and sighed;
    And silence followed after.

A Valentine

And cannot pleasures, while they last,
Be actual unless, when past,
They leave us shuddering and aghast,
    With anguish smarting?
And cannot friends be firm and fast,
    And yet bear parting?

And must I then, at Friendship's call,
Calmly resign the little all
(Trifling, I grant, it is and small)
    I have of gladness,
And lend my being to the thrall
    Of gloom and sadness?

And think you that I should be dumb,
And full *dolorum omnium*,
Excepting when *you* choose to come
    And share my dinner?
At other times be sour and glum,
    And daily thinner?

Must he then only live to weep,
Who'd prove his friendship true and deep,
By day a lonely shadow creep,
    At night rest badly,
Oft muttering in his broken sleep
    The name of Radley?

The lover, if for certain days
His fair one be denied his gaze,

Sinks not in grief and wild amaze,
    But, wiser wooer,
He spends the time in writing lays,
    And posts them to her.

And if he be an Oxford Don
Or 'Johnson's learned sock be on,'
A touching Valentine anon
    The post shall carry,
When thirteen days are come and gone
    Of February.

Farewell, dear friend, and when we meet,
In desert waste or crowded street,
Perhaps before this week shall fleet,
    Perhaps to-morrow.
I trust to find your heart the seat
    Of wasting sorrow.

A Sea Dirge

There are certain things – as, a spider, a ghost,
　　　The income-tax, gout, an umbrella for three –
That I hate, but the thing that I hate the most
　　　Is a thing they call the Sea.

Pour some salt water over the floor –
　　　Ugly I'm sure you'll allow it to be:
Suppose it extended a mile or more,
　　　That's very like the Sea.

Beat a dog till it howls outright –
　　　Cruel, but all very well for a spree:
Suppose that he did so day and night,
　　　That would be like the Sea.

I had a vision of nursery-maids;
　　　Tens of thousands passed by me –
All leading children with wooden spades,
　　　And this was by the Sea.

Who invented those spades of wood?
　　　Who was it cut them out of the tree?
None, I think, but an idiot could –
　　　Or one that loved the Sea.

It is pleasant and dreamy, no doubt, to float
　　　With 'thoughts as boundless, and souls as free'!
But, suppose you are very unwell in the boat,
　　　How do you like the Sea?

'But it makes the intellect clear and keen —'
    Prove it! Prove it! How can it be?
'Why, what does "B sharp" (in music) mean.
    If not the "natural C"?'

What, keen? With such questions as 'When's high tide?
    Is shelling shrimps an improvement to tea?
Are donkeys adapted for Man to ride?'
    Such are our thoughts by the Sea.

There is an insect that people avoid
    (Whence is derived the verb 'to flee');
Where have you been by it most annoyed?
    In lodgings by the Sea.

If you like your coffee with sand for dregs,
    A decided hint of salt in your tea,
And a fishy taste in the very eggs —
    By all means choose the Sea.

And if, with these dainties to drink and eat,
    You prefer not a vestige of grass or tree,
And a chronic state of wet in your feet,
    Then — I recommend the Sea.

For I have friends who dwell by the coast —
    Pleasant friends they are to me!
It is when I am with them I wonder most
    That anyone likes the Sea.

They take me a walk: though tired and stiff,
    To climb the heights I madly agree;

And, after a tumble or so from the cliff,
  They kindly suggest the Sea.

I try the rocks, and I think it cool
  That they laugh with such an excess of glee,
As I heavily slip into every pool
  That skirts the cold cold Sea.

Once I met a friend in the street,
  With wife, and nurse, and children three –
Never again such a sight may I meet
  As that party from the Sea!

Their looks were sullen, their steps were slow,
  Convicted felons they seemed to be:
'Are you going to prison, dear friend?' 'Oh no!
  We're returning – from the Sea!'

Atalanta in Camden Town

Ay, 'twas here, on this spot,
    In that summer of yore,
Atalanta did not
    Vote my presence a bore,
Nor reply, to my tenderest talk, she had 'heard all that
  nonsense before.'

She'd the brooch I had bought
    And the necklace and sash on,
And her heart, as I thought,
    Was alive to my passion;
And she'd done up her hair in the style that the Empress
  had brought into fashion.

I had been to the play
    With my pearl of a Peri –
But, for all I could say,
    She declared she was weary,
That 'the place was so crowded and hot', and she
  'couldn't abide that Dundreary.'

Then I thought ''Tis for me
    That she whines and she whimpers!'
And it soothed me to see
    Those sensational simpers:
And I said 'This is scrumptious!' – a phrase I had learned
  from the Devonshire shrimpers.

And I vowed ''Twill be said
    I'm a fortunate fellow,

When the breakfast is spread,
          When the topers are mellow,
When the foam of the bride-cake is white,
     and the fierce orange-blossoms are yellow.'

          O that languishing yawn!
               O those eloquent eyes!
          I was drunk with the dawn
               Of a splendid surmise –
I was stung by a look, I was slain by a tear,
     by a tempest of sighs.

          And I whispered 'I guess
               The sweet secret thou keepest,
          And the dainty distress
               That thou wistfully weepest;
And the question is "License or banns?", though undoubt-
     edly banns are the cheapest.'

          Then her white hand I clasped,
               And with kisses I crowned it:
          But she glared and she gasped,
               And she muttered 'Confound it!' –
Or at least it was something like that, but the noise
          Of the omnibus drowned it.

Phantasmagoria

CANTO I
The Trystyng

One winter night, at half-past nine,
    Cold, tired, and cross, and muddy,
I had come home, too late to dine,
And supper, with cigars and wine,
    Was waiting in the study.

There was a strangeness in the room,
    And something white and wavy
Was standing near me in the gloom –
I took it for the carpet-broom
    Left by that careless slavey.

But presently the thing began
    To shiver and to sneeze:
On which I said 'Come, come, my man,
That's a most inconsiderate plan –
    Less noise there, if you please!'

'I've caught a cold,' the thing replies,
    'Out there upon the landing –'
I turned to look in some surprise,
And there, before my very eyes,
    A little Ghost was standing!

He trembled when he caught my eye,
    And got behind a chair:
'How came you here,' I said, 'and why?

I never saw a thing so shy.
  Come out! Don't shiver there!'

He said 'I'd gladly tell you how,
  And also tell you why,
But' (here he gave a little bow)
'You're in so bad a temper now,
  You'd think it all a lie.

'And as to being in a fright,
  Allow me to remark
That ghosts have just as good a right
In every way, to fear the light,
  As men to fear the dark.'

'No plea,' said I, 'can well excuse
  Such cowardice in you:
For ghosts can visit when they choose,
Whereas we humans can't refuse
  To grant the interview.'

He said 'A flutter of alarm
  Is not unnatural, is it?
I really feared you meant some harm,
But, now I see that you are calm,
  Let me explain my visit.

'That last ghost left you on the third –
  Since then you've not been haunted:
But, as he never sent us word,
'Twas quite by accident we heard
  That any one was wanted.

'A Spectre has first choice, by right,
        In filling up a vacancy;
Then Phantom, Goblin, Elf, and Sprite —
If all these fail them, they invite
        The nicest Ghoul that they can see.

'The Spectres said the place was low,
        And that you kept bad wine:
So, as a Phantom had to go,
And I was first, of course, you know,
        I couldn't well decline.'

'No doubt,' said I, 'they settled who
        Was fittest to be sent:
Yet still to choose a brat like you,
To haunt a man of forty-two,
        Was no great compliment.'

'I'm not so young, Sir,' he replied,
        'As you might think — the fact is,
In caverns by the water-side,
And other places that I've tried,
        I've had a lot of practice:

'But I have never taken yet
        A strict domestic part,
And in my flurry I forget
The Five Good Rules of Etiquette
        We have to know by heart.'

My sympathies were warming fast
    Towards the little fellow:
He was so very much aghast
At having found a man at last,
    And looked so scared and yellow.

'At least,' I said, 'I'm glad to find
    A ghost is not a dumb thing –
But pray sit down – you'll feel inclined
(If, like myself, you have not dined)
    To take a snack of something:

'(Though, certainly, you don't appear
    A thing to offer food to);
And then I shall be glad to hear
(If you will say them loud and clear)
    The rules that you allude to.'

'Thanks! You shall hear them by and by –
    This is a piece of luck!'
'What may I offer you?' said I.
'Well, since you are so kind, I'll try
    A little bit of duck.

'One slice! And may I ask you for
    A little drop of gravy?'
I sat and looked at him in awe,
For certainly I never saw
    A thing so white and wavy.

And still he seemed to grow more white,
      More vapoury, and wavier –
Seen in the dim and flickering light,
As he proceeded to recite
      His 'Maxims of Behaviour.'

CANTO II
Hys Fyve Rules

'My First – but don't suppose,' he said,
      'I'm setting you a riddle –
Is – if your Victim be in bed,
Don't touch the curtains at his head,
      But take it in the middle,

'And wave it slowly to and fro,
      As if the wind was at it;
And in a minute's time or so
He'll be awake – and this you'll know
      By hearing him say *"Drat it!"*

'(And here you must on no pretence
      Make the first observation:
Wait for the Victim to commence –
No ghost of any common sense
      Begins a conversation.)

'If he should say *"How came you here?"*
      (The way that *you* began, Sir),
In such a case your course is clear –
'Just as you please, my little dear!'
      Or any other answer.

'But if the wrtech says nothing more,
        You'd best perhaps curtail your
Exertions – go and shake the door,
And then, if he begins to snore,
        You'll know the thing's a failure.

'By day, if he should be alone –
        At home or on a walk –
You merely give a hollow groan,
To indicate the kind of tone
        In which you mean to talk.

'But if you find him with his friends,
        The thing is rather harder.
In such a case success depends
On picking up some candle-ends,
        Or butter, in the larder.

'With this you make a kind of slide
        (It answers best with suet),
On which you must contrive to glide,
And swing yourself from side to side –
        One soon learns how to do it.

'The Second tells us what is right
        In ceremonious calls:
"First burn a blue or crimson light"
(A thing I quite forgot to-night),
        "Then scratch the door or walls."'

I said 'You'll visit here no more,
        If you attempt the Guy:

I'll have no bonfires on my floor —
And, as for scratching at the door,
    I'd like to see you try!'

'The Third was written to protect
    The interests of the Victim,
And tells us, as I recollect,
To treat him with a grave respect,
    And not to contradict him.'

'That's plain,' said I, 'as Tare and Tret,
    To any comprehension:
I only wish some ghosts I've met
Would not so constantly forget
    The maxim that you mention.'

'Perhaps,' he said, 'you first transgressed
    The laws of hospitality:
You'll mostly come off second-best
When you omit to treat your guest
    With proper cordiality.

'If you address a ghost as "thing,"
    Or strike him with a hatchet,
He is permitted by the king
To drop all formal parleying —
    And then you're sure to catch it!

'The Fourth prohibits trespassing
    Where other ghosts are quartered:

And those convicted of the thing
(Unless when pardoned by the king)
     Must instantly be slaughtered.'

I said 'That rule appears to me
     Wanting in common sense –'
'"To slaughter" does not mean,' said he,
'"To kill" with us, and that, you see,
     Makes a *great* difference.

'In fact we're simply cut up small;
     (Ghosts soon unite anew;)
The process scarcely hurts at all,
Not more than when *you*'re what you call
     "Cut up" by a Review.

'The Fifth is one you may prefer
     That I should quote entire –
The King must be addressed as "Sir":
This, from a simple courtier,
     Is all the Laws require:

'*But, should you wish to do the thing*
     With out-and-out politeness,
Accost him as "My Goblin King!"
And always use, in answering,
     The phrase "Your Royal Whiteness!"

'I'm getting rather hoarse, I fear,
     After so much reciting;

So, if you don't object, my dear,
We'll try a glass of bitter beer –
　　　I think it looks inviting.'

CANTO III
Scarmoges

'And did you really walk,' said I,
　　　'On such a wretched night?
I always fancied ghosts could fly –
If not exactly in the sky,
　　　Yet at a fairish height.'

'It's very well,' said he, 'for kings
　　　To fly above the earth:
But Phantoms often find that wings,
Like many other pleasant things,
　　　Cost more than they are worth.

'Spectres of course are rich, and so
　　　Can buy them from the Elves:
But *we* prefer to keep below –
They're stupid company, you know,
　　　For any but themselves.

'For, though they claim to be exempt
　　　From pride, they treat a Phantom
As something quite beneath contempt –
(Just as no turkey ever dreamt
　　　Of noticing a Bantam).'

'They seem too proud,' said I, 'to go
        To houses such as mine –
Pray, how did they contrive to know
So quickly that "the place was low,"
        And that I "kept bad wine"?'

'Inspector Kobold called on you –'
        The little ghost began:
Here I broke in; 'Inspector who?
Inspecting ghosts is something new:
        Explain yourself, my man!'

'His name is Kobold,' said my guest,
        'One of the Spectre order:
You'll very often see him dressed
In a yellow gown, a crimson vest,
        And a night-cap with a border.

'He tried the Brocken business first,
        But caught a sort of chill;
So came to England to be nursed,
And here it took the form of thirst,
        Which he complains of still.

'The remedy, *he says*, is port,
        (Which he compares to nectar,)
And, as the inns where it is brought,
Have always been his chief resort,
        We call him the "*Inn-Spectre*."'

I bear it well as any man
    The washiest of witticism;
And nothing could be sweeter than
My temper, till the ghost began
    Some most provoking criticisms.

'Cooks need not be indulged in waste,
    Yet still you'd better teach them
Dishes should have *some sort* of taste –
Pray, why are all the cruets placed
    Where nobody can reach them?

'That man of yours will never earn
    His living as a waiter –
Is that queer thing supposed to burn?
(It's far too dismal a concern
    To call a Moderator).

'The duck was tender, but the peas
    Were very much too old:
And just remember, if you please,
The next time you have toasted cheese,
    Don't let them send it cold.

'You'd find the bread improved, I think,
    By getting better flour:
And have you anything to drink
That looks a little less like ink,
    And isn't quite so sour?'

Then, peering round with curious eyes,
	He muttered 'Goodness gracious!'
And so went on to criticise –
'Your room's an inconvenient size;
	It's neither snug nor spacious.

'That narrow window, I expect,
	Serves but to let the dusk in –'
I cried 'But please to recollect
'Twas fashioned by an architect
	Who pinned his faith on Ruskin!'

'I don't care who he was, Sir, or
	On whom he pinned his faith!
Constructed by whatever law,
So poor a job I never saw,
	As I'm a living Wraith!

'What a re-markable cigar!
	How much are they a dozen?'
I growled 'No matter what they are!
You're getting as familiar
	As if you were my cousin!

'Now that's a thing I will not stand,
	And so I tell you flat –'
'Aha,' said he, 'We're getting grand!'
(Taking a bottle in his hand,)
	'I'll soon arrange for that!'

And here he took a careful aim,
　　And gaily cried 'Here goes!'
I tried to dodge it as it came,
But somehow caught it, all the same,
　　Exactly on my nose.

And I remember nothing more
　　That I can clearly fix,
Till I was sitting on the floor,
Repeating 'Two and five are four,
　　But *three and two* are six.'

What really passed I never learned,
　　Nor guessed: I only know
That, when at last my sense returned,
The lamp, neglected, dimly burned –
　　The fire was getting low –

Through driving mists I seemed to see
　　A form of sheet and bone –
And found that he was telling me
The whole of his biography,
　　In a familiar tone.

CANTO IV
Hys Nouryture

'Oh, when I was a little Ghost,
　　A merry time had we!
Each seated on his favourite post,
We chumped and chawed the buttered toast
　　They gave us for our tea.'

'That story is in print!' I cried.
        'Don't say it's not, because
It's known as well as Bradshaw's Guide!'
(The ghost uneasily replied
        He hardly thought it was.)

'It's not in Nursery Rhymes? And yet
        I almost think it is —
"Three little ghostesses" were set
"On postesses," you know, and ate
        Their "buttered toastesses."

'I have the book; so if you doubt it —'
        I turned to search the shelf.
'Don't stir!' he cried. 'We'll do without it:
I now remember all about it;
        I wrote the thing myself.

'It came out in a "Monthly," or
        At least my agent said it did:
Some literary swell, who saw
It, thought it seemed adapted for
        The Magazine he edited.

'My father was a Brownie, Sir;
        My mother was a Fairy.
The notion had occurred to her,
The children would be happier,
        If they were taught to vary.

'The notion soon became a craze;
        And, when it once began, she

Brought us all out in different ways –
One was a Pixy, two were Fays,
      Another was a Banshee;

'The Fetch and Kelpie went to school
      And gave a lot of trouble;
Next came a Poltergeist and Ghoul,
And then two Trolls (which broke the rule),
      A Goblin, and a Double –

'(If that's a snuff-box on the shelf,'
      He added with a yawn,
'I'll take a pinch) – next came an Elf,
And then a Phantom (that's myself),
      And last, a Leprechaun.

'One day, some Spectres chanced to call,
      Dressed in the usual white:
I stood and watched them in the hall,
And couldn't make them out at all,
      They seemed so strange a sight:

'I wondered what on earth they were,
      That looked all head and sack;
But mother told me not to stare,
And then she twitched me by the hair,
      And punched me in the back.

'Since then I've often wished that I
      Had been a Spectre born.
But what's the use?' (He heaved a sigh.)

'They are the ghost-nobility,
      And look on us with scorn.

'My phantom-life was soon begun:
      When I was barely six,
I went out with an older one –
And just at first I thought it fun,
      And went at it like bricks.

'I've haunted dungeons, castles, towers –
      Wherever I was sent:
I've often sat and howled for hours,
Drenched to the skin with driving showers,
      Upon a battlement.

'It's quite old-fashioned now to groan
      When you begin to speak:
This is the newest thing in tone –'
And here (it chilled me to the bone)
      He gave an awful squeak.

'Perhaps,' he added, 'to your ear
      That sounds an easy thing?
Try it yourself, my little dear!
It took me something like a year,
      With constant practising.

'And when you've learned to squeak, my man,
      And caught the double sob,
You're pretty much where you began –
Just try and gibber if you can!
      That's something like a job!

'I've tried it, and can only say
    I'm sure you couldn't do it, e-
ven if you practised night and day,
Unless you have a turn that way,
    And natural ingenuity.

'Shakespeare I think it is who treats
    Of Ghosts, in days of old,
Who "gibbered in the Roman streets,"
Dressed, if you recollect, in sheets –
    They must have found it cold.

'I've often spent ten pounds on stuff,
    In dressing as a Double,
But, though it answers as a puff,
It never has effect enough
    To make it worth the trouble.

'Long bills soon quenched the little thirst
    I had for being funny –
The setting-up is always worst:
Such heaps of things you want at first,
    One must be made of money!

'For instance, take a haunted tower,
    With skull, cross-bones, and sheet;
Blue lights to burn (say) two an hour,
Condensing lens of extra power,
    And set of chains complete:

'What with the things you have to hire –
    The fitting on the robe –

And testing all the coloured fire –
The outfit of itself would tire
    The patience of a Job!

'And then they're so fastidious,
    The Haunted-House Committee:
I've often known them make a fuss
Because a ghost was French, or Russ,
    Or even from the City!

'Some dialects are objected to –
    For one, the Irish brogue is:
And then, for all you have to do,
One pound a week they offer you,
    And find yourself in Bogies!'

CANTO V
Byckerment

'Don't they consult the "Victims," though?'
    I said. 'They should, by rights,
Give them a chance – because, you know,
The tastes of people differ so,
    Especially in Sprites.'

The Phantom shook his head and smiled.
    'Consult them? Not a bit!
'Twould be a job to drive one wild,
To satisfy one single child –
    There'd be no end to it!'

'Of course you can't leave children free,'
    Said I, 'to pick and choose:

But, in the case of men like me,
I think "Mine Host" might fairly be
      Allowed to state his views.'

He said 'It really wouldn't pay –
      Folk are so full of fancies.
We visit for a single day,
And whether then we go, or stay,
      Depends on circumstances.

'And, though we don't consult "Mine Host"
      Before the thing's arranged,
Still, if the tenant quits his post,
Or is not a well-mannered ghost,
      Then you can have him changed.

'But if the host's a man like you –
      I mean a man of sense;
And if the house is not too new –'
'Why, what has that,' said I, 'to do
      With ghost's convenience?'

'A new house does not suit, you know –
      It's such a job to trim it:
But, after twenty years or so,
The wainscotings begin to go,
      So twenty is the limit.'

'To trim' was not a phrase I could
      Remember having heard:
'Perhaps,' I said, 'you'll be so good

As tell me what is understood
        Exactly by that word?'

'It means the loosening all the doors,'
        The ghost replied, and laughed:
'It means the drilling holes by scores
In all the skirting-boards and floors,
        To make a thorough draught.

'You'll sometimes find that one or two
        Are all you really need
To let the wind come whistling through –
But here there'll be a lot to do!'
        I faintly gasped 'Indeed!

'If I'd been rather later, I'll
        Be bound,' I added, trying
(Most unsuccessfully) to smile,
'You'd have been busy all this while,
        Trimming and beautifying?'

'Why, no,' said he; 'perhaps I should
        Have stayed another minute –
But still no ghost, that's any good,
Without an introduction would
        Have ventured to begin it.

'The proper thing, as you were late,
        Was certainly to go:
But, with the roads in such a state,
I got the Knight-Mayor's leave to wait
        For half an hour or so.'

'Who's the Knight-Mayor?' I cried. Instead
    Of answering my question,
'Well, if you don't know *that*,' he said,
'Either you never go to bed,
    Or you've a grand digestion!

'He goes about and sits on folk
    That eat too much at night:
His duties are to "pinch, and poke,
And squeeze them till they nearly choke."'
    (I said 'It serves them right!')

'And folk who sup on things like these –'
    He muttered, 'eggs and bacon –
Lobster – and duck – and toasted cheese –
If they don't get an awful squeeze,
    I'm very much mistaken!

'He is immensely fat, and so
    Well suits the occupation:
In point of fact, if you must know,
We used to call him years ago,
    "The Mayor and Corporation"!

'The day he was elected Mayor
    I *know* that every Sprite meant
To vote for *me*, but did not dare –
He was so frantic with despair
    And furious with excitement.

'When it was over, for a whim,
        He ran to tell the king;
And being the reverse of slim,
A two-mile trot was not for him
        A very easy thing.

'So, to reward him for his run
        (As it was baking hot,
And he was over twenty stone,)
The king proceeded, half in fun,
        To knight him on the spot.'

''Twas a great liberty to take!'
        (I fired up like a rocket.)
'He did it just for punning's sake –
"The man," says Johnson, "that would make
        A pun, would pick a pocket!"'

'A man,' said he, 'is not a king.'
        I argued for a while,
And did my best to prove the thing –
The Phantom merely listening
        With a contemptuous smile.

At last, when, breath and patience spent,
        I had recourse to smoking –
'Your aim,' he said, 'is excellent:
But – when you call it argument –
        Of course you're only joking?'

Stung by his cold and snaky eye,
        I roused myself at length
To say 'At least I do defy
The veriest sceptic to deny
        That union is strength!'

'That's true enough,' said he, 'yet stay –'
        I listened in all meekness –
'Union is strength, I'm bound to say;
In fact, the thing's as clear as day;
        But onions – are a weakness.'

CANTO VI
Dyscomfyture

As one who strives a hill to climb,
        Who never climbed before:
Who finds it, in a little time,
Grow every moment less sublime,
        And votes the thing a bore:

Yet, having once begun to try,
        Dares not desert his quest,
But, climbing, ever keeps his eye
On one small hut against the sky,
        Wherein he hopes to rest:

Who climbs till nerve and force be spent,
        With many a puff and pant:
Who still, as rises the ascent,
In language grows more violent,
        Although in breath more scant:

Who, climbing, gains at length the place
        That crowns the upward track;
And, entering with unsteady pace,
Receives a buffet in the face
        That lands him on his back:

And feels himself, like one in sleep,
        Glide swiftly down again,
A helpless weight, from steep to steep,
Till, with a headlong giddy sweep,
        He drops upon the plain –

So I, that had resolved to bring
        Conviction to a ghost,
And found it quite a different thing
From any human arguing,
        Yet dared not quit my post:

But, keeping still the end in view
        To which I hoped to come,
I strove to prove the matter true
By putting everything I knew
        Into an axiom:

Commencing every single phrase
        With 'therefore' or 'because,'
I blindly reeled, a hundred ways,
About the syllogistic maze,
        Unconscious where I was.

Quoth he 'That's regular clap-trap –
        Don't bluster any more.

Now *do* be cool and take a nap!
You're such a peppery old chap
  As never was before!

'You're like a man I used to meet,
  Who got one day so furious
In arguing, the simple heat
Scorched both his slippers off his feet!'
  I said *'That's very curious!'*

'Well, it *is* curious, I agree,
  And sounds perhaps like fibs:
But still it's true as true can be –
As sure as your name's Tibbs,' said he.
  I said 'My name's *not* Tibbs.'

'*Not* Tibbs!' he cried – his tone became
  A shade or two less hearty –
'Why, no,' said I. 'My proper name
Is Tibbets –' 'Tibbets?' 'Aye, the same.'
  'Why, then YOU'RE NOT THE PARTY!'

With that he struck the board a blow
  That shivered half the glasses;
'Why couldn't you have told me so
Three quarters of an hour ago?
  You king of all the asses!

'To walk four miles through mud and rain,
  To spend the night in smoking,
And then to find that it's in vain –

And I've to do it all again –
    It's really *too* provoking!

'Don't talk!' he cried, as I began
    To mutter some excuse.
'Who can have patience with a man
That's got no more discretion than
    An idiotic goose?

'To keep me waiting here, instead
    Of telling me at once
That this was not the house!' he said.
'There, that'll do – be off to bed!
    Don't gape like that, you dunce!'

'It's very fine to throw the blame
    On *me* in such a fashion!
Why didn't you enquire my name
The very minute that you came?'
    I answered in a passion.

'Of course it worries you a bit
    To come so far on foot –
But how was I to blame for it?'
'Well, well!' said he. 'I must admit
    That isn't badly put.

'And certainly you've given me
    The best of wine and victual –
Excuse my violence,' said he,
'But accidents like this, you see,
    They put one out a little.

'"Twas my fault after all, I find –
　　　Shake hands, old Turnip-top!'
The name was hardly to my mind,
But, as no doubt he meant it kind,
　　　I let the matter drop.

'Good-night, old Turnip-top, good-night!
　　　When I am gone, perhaps
They'll send you some inferior Sprite,
Who'll keep you in a constant fright
　　　And spoil your soundest naps.

'Tell him you'll stand no sort of trick;
　　　Then, if he leers and chuckles,
You just be handy with a stick,
(Mind that it's pretty hard and thick,)
　　　And rap him on the knuckles!

'Then carelessly remark "Old coon!
　　　Perhaps you're not aware
That, if you don't behave, you'll soon
Be chuckling to another tune –
　　　And so you'd best take care!"

'That's the right way to cure a Sprite
　　　Of such-like goings-on –
But gracious me! It's nearly light!
Good-night, old Turnip-top, good-night!'
　　　A nod, and he was gone.

CANTO VII
Sad Souvenaunce

'What's this?' I pondered. 'Have I slept?
    Or can I have been drinking?'
But soon a gentler feeling crept
Upon me, and I sat and wept
    An hour or so, like winking.

Then, as my tears could never bring
    My favourite phantom back,
It seemed to me the proper thing
To mix another glass, and sing
    The following Coronach.

Coronach

'And art thou gone, beloved ghost?
    Best of familiars!
Nay then, farewell, my duckling roast,
Farewell, farewell, my tea and toast,
    My meerschaum and cigars!

'The hues of life are dull and grey,
    The sweets of life insipid,
When thou, my charmer, art away —
Old brick, or rather, let me say,
    Old parallelepiped!'

Instead of singing verse the third,
    I ceased; abruptly, rather —
But, after such a splendid word,

I felt that it would be absurd
    To try it any farther.

'No need for Bones to hurry so!'
    Thought I. 'In fact, I doubt
If it was worth his while to go –
And who is Tibbs, I'd like to know,
    To make such work about?

'If Tibbs is anything like me,
    It's *possible*,' I said,
'He won't be over-pleased to be
Dropped in upon at half-past three,
    After he's snug in bed.

'And if Bones plagues him anyhow –
    Squeaking and all the rest of it,
As he was doing here just now –
I prophesy there'll be a row,
    And Tibbs will have the best of it!'

So with a yawn I went my way
    To seek the welcome downy,
And slept, and dreamed till break of day
Of Poltergeist and Fetch and Fay
    And Leprechaun and Brownie!

And never since, by sea or land,
    On mountain or on plain,
'Mid Arctic snow, or Afric sand –
Not even 'in the Strand, the Strand!'
    Has Bones appeared again.

A Quaker friend accosted me –
      Tall, stiff, as any column –
'Thee'rt out of sorts, I fear,' said he;
'Verily I am grieved to see
      Thee go'st so grave and solemn.'

'The ghost's not grave,' I said, 'but gay;
      Not solemn, but convivial:
I'm "out of spirits," you should say,
Not "out of sorts" –' he turned away,
      Thinking the answer trivial.

For years I've not been visited
      By any kind of Sprite;
Yet still they echo in my head,
Those parting words, so kindly said,
      'Old Turnip-top, good-night!'

Four Riddles

There was an ancient City, stricken down
    With a strange frenzy, and for many a day
They paced from morn to eve the crowded town,
    And danced the night away.

I asked the cause: the aged man grew sad –
    They pointed to a building grey and tall,
And hoarsely answered 'Step inside, my lad,
    And then you'll see it all.'

Yet what are all such gaieties to me
    Whose thoughts are full of indices and surds?

$$x*x + 7x + 53 = 11/3$$

But something whispered 'It will soon be done –
    Bands cannot always play, nor ladies smile:
Endure with patience the distasteful fun
    For just a little while!'

A change came o'er my Vision – it was night:
    We clove a pathway through a frantic throng:
The steeds, wild-plunging, filled us with affright;
    The chariots whirled along.

Within a marble hall a river ran –
    A living tide, half muslin and half cloth:
And here one mourned a broken wreath or fan,
    Yet swallowed down her wrath;

And here one offered to a thirsty fair
    (His words half-drowned amid those thunders
        tuneful)
Some frozen viand (there were many there),
    A tooth-ache in each spoonful.

There comes a happy pause, for human strength
    Will not endure to dance without cessation;
And every one must reach the point at length
    Of absolute prostration.

At such a moment ladies learn to give,
    To partners who would urge them over-much,
A flat and yet decided negative –
    Photographers love such.

There comes a welcome summons – hope revives,
    And fading eyes grow bright, and pulses quicken:
Incessant pop the corks, and busy knives
    Dispense the tongue and chicken.

Flushed with new life, the crowd flows back again:
    And all is tangled talk and mazy motion –
Much like a waving field of golden grain,
    Or a tempestuous ocean.

And thus they give the time, that Nature meant
    For peaceful sleep and meditative snores,
To thoughtless din, and mindless merriment,
    And waste of shoes and floors.

And one (we name him not) that flies the flowers,
 That dreads the dances, and that shuns the salads,
They doom to pass in solitude the hours,
 Writing acrostic-ballads.

How late it grows! The hour is surely past
 That should have warned us with its double knock;
The twilight wanes, and morning comes at last –
 'Oh, Uncle, what's o'clock?'

The Uncle gravely nods, and wisely winks.
 It may mean much; but how is one to know?
He opens his mouth – yet out of it, methinks,
 No words of wisdom flow.

II

Empress of Art, for thee I twine
This wreath with all too slender skill.
Forgive my Muse each halting line,
And for the deed accept the will!

O day of tears! Whence comes this spectre grim,
Parting, like Death's cold river, souls that love?
Is not he bound to thee, as thou to him,
By vows, unwhispered here, yet heard above?

And still it lives, that keen and heavenward flame,
Lives in his eye, and trembles in his tone:
And these wild words of fury but proclaim
A heart that beats for thee, for thee alone!

But all is lost: that mighty mind o'erthrown,
Like sweet bells jangled, piteous sight to see!
'Doubt that the stars are fire,' so runs his moan,
'Doubt Truth herself, but not my love for thee!'

A sadder vision yet: thine aged sire
Shaming his hoary locks with treacherous wile!
And dost thou now doubt Truth to be a liar?
And wilt thou die, that hast forgot to smile?

Nay, get thee hence! Leave all thy winsome ways
And the faint fragrance of thy scattered flowers:
In holy silence wait the appointed days,
And weep away the leaden-footed hours.

III

The air is bright with hues of light
And rich with laughter and with singing:
Young hearts beat high in ecstasy,
And banners wave, and bells are ringing:
But silence falls with fading day,
And there's an end to mirth and play.
Ah, well-a-day!

Rest your old bones, ye wrinkled crones!
The kettle sings, the firelight dances.
Deep be it quaffed, the magic draught
That fills the soul with golden fancies!
For Youth and Pleasance will not stay,
And ye are withered, worn, and grey.
Ah, well-a-day!
O fair cold face! O form of grace,

For human passion madly yearning!
O weary air of dumb despair,
From marble won, to marble turning!
'Leave us not thus!' we fondly pray.
'We cannot let thee pass away!'
Ah, well-a-day!

IV

My First is singular at best:
More plural is my Second:
My Third is far the pluralest –
So plural-plural, I protest
It scarcely can be reckoned!

My First is followed by a bird:
My Second by believers
In magic art: my simple Third
Follows, too often, hopes absurd
And plausible deceivers.

My First to get at wisdom tries –
A failure melancholy!
My Second men revered as wise:
My Third from heights of wisdom flies
To depths of frantic folly.

My First is ageing day by day:
My Second's age is ended:
My Third enjoys an age, they say,
That never seems to fade away,
Through centuries extended.
My Whole? I need a poet's pen

To paint her myriad phases:
The monarch, and the slave, of men –
A mountain-summit, and a den
Of dark and deadly mazes –

A flashing light – a fleeting shade –
Beginning, end, and middle
Of all that human art hath made
Or wit devised! Go, seek HER aid,
If you would read my riddle!

A Game of Fives

Five little girls, of Five, Four, Three, Two, One:
Rolling on the hearthrug, full of tricks and fun.
Five rosy girls, in years from Ten to Six:
Sitting down to lessons – no more time for tricks.

Five growing girls, from Fifteen to Eleven:
Music, Drawing, Languages, and food enough for seven!
Five winsome girls, from Twenty to Sixteen:
Each young man that calls, I say 'Now tell me which you
    mean!'
Five dashing girls, the youngest Twenty-one:
But, if nobody proposes, what is there to be done?

Five showy girls – but Thirty is an age
When girls may be *engaging*, but they somehow don't *engage*.
Five dressy girls, of Thirty-one or more:
So gracious to the shy young men they snubbed so much
    before!

Five *passé* girls – Their age? Well, never mind!
We jog along together, like the rest of human kind:
But the quondam 'careless bachelor' begins to think he
    knows
The answer to that ancient problem 'how the money
    goes'!

Poeta Fit Non Nascitur

'How shall I be a poet?
  How shall I write in rhyme?
You told me once "the very wish
  Partook of the sublime:"
Then tell me how! Don't put me off
  With your "another time"!'

The old man smiled to see him,
  To hear his sudden sally;
He liked the lad to speak his mind
  Enthusiastically;
And thought 'There's no hum-drum in him,
  Nor any shilly-shally.'

'And would you be a poet
  Before you've been to school?
Ah, well! I hardly thought you
  So absolute a fool.
First learn to be spasmodic –
  A very simple rule.

'For first you write a sentence,
  And then you chop it small;
Then mix the bits, and sort them out
  Just as they chance to fall:
The order of the phrases makes
  No difference at all.

'Then, if you'd be impressive,
  Remember what I say,

That abstract qualities begin
  With capitals alway:
The True, the Good, the Beautiful —
  Those are the things that pay!

'Next, when you are describing
  A shape, or sound, or tint;
Don't state the matter plainly,
  But put it in a hint;
And learn to look at all things
  With a sort of mental squint.'

'For instance, if I wished, Sir,
  Of mutton-pies to tell,
Should I say "dreams of fleecy flocks
  Pent in a wheaten cell"?'
'Why, yes,' the old man said: 'that phrase
  Would answer very well.

'Then fourthly, there are epithets
  That suit with any word —
As well as Harvey's Reading Sauce
  With fish, or flesh, or bird —
Of these, "wild," "lonely," "weary," "strange,"
  Are much to be preferred.'

'And will it do, O will it do
  To take them in a lump —
As "the wild man went his weary way
  To a strange and lonely pump"?'
'Nay, nay! You must not hastily
  To such conclusions jump.

'Such epithets, like pepper,
    Give zest to what you write;
And, if you strew them sparely,
    They whet the appetite:
But if you lay them on too thick,
    You spoil the matter quite!

'Last, as to the arrangement:
    Your reader, you should show him,
Must take what information he
    Can get, and look for no im-
mature disclosure of the drift
    And purpose of your poem.

'Therefore, to test his patience –
    How much he can endure –
Mention no places, names, or dates,
    And evermore be sure
Throughout the poem to be found
    Consistently obscure.

'First fix upon the limit
    To which it shall extend:
Then fill it up with "Padding" –
    (Beg some of any friend):
Your great SENSATION-STANZA
    You place towards the end.'

'And what is a Sensation,
    Grandfather, tell me, pray?
I think I never heard the word
    So used before to-day:

Be kind enough to mention one
    "*Exempli gratiâ.*"'

And the old man, looking sadly
    Across the garden-lawn,
Where here and there a dew-drop
    Yet glittered in the dawn,
Said 'Go to the Adelphi,
    And see the 'Colleen Bawn.'

'The word is due to Boucicault –
    The theory is his,
Where Life becomes a spasm,
    And History a whiz:
If that is not Sensation,
    I don't know what it is.

'Now try your hand, ere Fancy
    Have lost its present glow –'
'And then,' his grandson added,
    'We'll publish it, you know:
Green cloth – gold-lettered at the back –
    In duodecimo!'

Then proudly smiled that old man
    To see the eager lad
Rush madly for his pen and ink
    And for his blotting-pad –
But, when he thought of publishing,
    His face grew stern and sad.

Ye Carpette Knyghte

I have a horse – a ryghte good horse –
    Ne doe I envie those
Who scoure ye plaine yn headie course,
    Tyll soddaine on theire nose
They lyghte wyth unexpected force –
    Yt ys – a horse of clothes.

I have a saddel – 'Say'st thou soe?
    Wyth styrruppes, Knyghte, to boote?'
I sayde not that – I answere 'Noe' –
    Yt lacketh such, I woot –
Yt ys a mutton-saddel, loe!
    Parte of ye fleecie brute.

I have a bytte – a ryghte good bytte –
    As schall bee seene yn tyme.
Ye jawe of horse yt wyll not fytte;
    Yts use ys more sublyme.
Fayre Syr, how deemest thou of yt?
    Yt ys – thys bytte of rhyme.

The Three Voices

The First Voice.

With hands tight clenched through matted hair,
He crouched in trance of dumb despair:
There came a breeze from out the air.

It passed athwart the glooming flat —
It fanned his forehead as he sat —
It lightly bore away his hat,

All to the feet of one who stood
Like maid enchanted in a wood,
Frowning as darkly as she could,

With huge umbrella, lank and brown,
Unerringly she pinned it down,
Right through the centre of the crown.

Then, with an aspect cold and grim,
Regardless of its battered rim,
She took it up and gave it him.

Awhile like one in dreams he stood,
Then faltered forth his gratitude,
In words just short of being rude:

For it had lost its shape and shine,
And it had cost him four-and-nine,
And he was going out to dine.

With grave indifference to his speech,
Fixing her eyes upon the beach,
She said 'Each gives to more than each.'

He could not answer yea or nay;
He faltered 'Gifts may pass away.'
Yet knew not what he meant to say.

'If that be so,' she straight replied,
'Each heart with each doth coincide:
What boots it? For the world is wide.'

And he, not wishing to appear
Less wise, said 'This Material Sphere
Is but Attributive Idea.'

But when she asked him 'Wherefore so?'
He felt his very whiskers glow,
And frankly owned 'I do not know.'

While, like broad waves of golden grain,
Or sunlit hues on cloistered pane,
His colour came and went again.

Pitying his obvious distress,
Yet with a tinge of bitterness,
She said 'The More exceeds the Less.'

'A truth of such undoubted weight,'
He urged, 'and so extreme in date,
It were superfluous to state.'

Roused into sudden passion, she
In tone of cold malignity:
'To others, yes; but not to thee.'

But when she saw him quail and quake,
And when he urged 'For pity's sake!'
Once more in gentle tone she spake:

'Thought in the mind doth still abide;
That is by Intellect supplied,
And within that Idea doth hide.

'And he, that yearns the truth to know,
Still further inwardly may go,
And find Idea from Notion flow.

'And thus the chain, that sages sought,
Is to a glorious circle wrought,
For Notion hath its source in Thought.'

When he, with racked and whirling brain,
Feebly implored her to explain,
She simply said it all again.

Wrenched with an agony intense,
He spake, neglecting Sound and Sense,
And careless of all consequence:

'Mind – I believe – is Essence – Ent –
Abstract – that is – an Accident –
Which we – that is to say – I meant –'

When, with quick breath and cheeks all flushed,
At length his speech was somewhat hushed,
She looked at him, and he was crushed.

It needed not her calm reply;
She fixed him with a stony eye,
And he could neither fight nor fly,

While she dissected, word by word,
His speech, half guessed at and half heard,
As might a cat a little bird.

Then, having wholly overthrown
His views, and stripped them to the bone,
Proceeded to unfold her own.

So passed they on with even pace,
Yet gradually one might trace
A shadow growing on his face.

The Second Voice.

They walked beside the wave-worn beach,
Her tongue was very apt to teach,
And now and then he did beseech

She would abate her dulcet tone,
Because the talk was all her own,
And he was dull as any drone.

She urged 'No cheese is made of chalk:'
And ceaseless flowed her dreary talk,
Tuned to the footfall of a walk.

Her voice was very full and rich,
And when at length she asked him 'Which?'
It mounted to its highest pitch.

He a bewildered answer gave,
Drowned in the sullen moaning wave,
Lost in the echoes of the cave.

He answered her he knew not what;
Like shaft from bow at random shot:
He spoke, but she regarded not.

She waited not for his reply,
But with a downward leaden eye
Went on as if he were not by.

Sound argument and grave defence,
Strange questions raised on 'Why?' and 'Whence?'
And weighted down with common sense.

'Shall Man be Man? and shall he miss
Of other thoughts no thought but this,
Harmonious dews of sober bliss?

'What boots it? Shall his fevered eye
Through towering nothingness descry
The grisly phantom hurry by?

'And hear dumb shrieks that fill the air;
See mouths that gape, and eyes that stare
And redden in the dusky glare?

'The meadows breathing amber light,
The darkness toppling from the height,
The feathery train of granite Night?

'Shall he, grown grey among his peers,
Through the thick curtain of his tears
Catch glimpses of his earlier years,

'And hear the sounds he knew of yore,
Old shufflings on the sanded floor,
Old knuckles tapping at the door?

'Yet still before him as he flies
One pallid form shall ever rise,
And, bodying forth in glassy eyes

'The vision of a vanished good,
Low peering through the tangled wood,
Shall freeze the current of his blood.'

Still from each fact, with skill uncouth
And savage rapture, like a tooth
She wrenched a slow reluctant truth.

Till, like some silent water-mill,
When summer suns have dried the rill,
She reached a full stop, and was still.

Dead calm succeeded to the fuss,
As when the loaded omnibus
Has reached the railway terminus;

When, for the tumult of the street
Is heard the engine's stifled beat,
The wary tread of porters' feet.

With glance that ever sought the ground,
She moved her lips without a sound,
And every now and then she frowned.

He gazed upon the sleeping sea,
And joyed in its tranquillity,
And in that silence dead, but she

To muse a little space did seem,
Then, like the echo of a dream,
Harped back upon her threadbare theme.

Still an attentive ear he lent,
But could not fathom what she meant:
She was not deep, nor eloquent.

He marked the ripple on the sand:
The even swaying of her hand
Was all that he could understand.

He left her, and he turned aside:
He sat and watched the coming tide
Across the shores so newly dried.

He wondered at the waters clear,
The breeze that whispered in his ear,
The billows heaving far and near;

And why he had so long preferred
To hang upon her every word;
'In truth,' he said, 'it was absurd.'

The Third Voice.

Not long this transport held its place:
Within a little moment's space
Quick tears were raining down his face.

His heart stood still, aghast with fear;
A wordless voice, nor far nor near,
He seemed to hear and not to hear.

'Tears kindle not the doubtful spark:
If so, why not? Of this remark
The bearings are profoundly dark.'

'Her speech,' he said, 'hath caused this pain;
Easier I count it to explain
The jargon of the howling main,

'Or, stretched beside some sedgy brook,
To con, with inexpressive look,
An unintelligible book.'

Low spake the voice within his head,
In words imagined more than said,
Soundless as ghost's intended tread:

'If thou art duller than before,
Why quittedst thou the voice of lore?
Why not endure, expecting more?'

'Rather than that,' he groaned aghast,
'I'd writhe in depths of cavern vast,
Some loathly vampire's rich repast.'

''Twere hard,' it answered, 'themes immense
To coop within the narrow fence
That rings thy scant intelligence.'

'Not so,' he urged, 'nor once alone:
But there was that within her tone
Which chilled me to the very bone.

'Her style was anything but clear,
And most unpleasantly severe;
Her epithets were very queer.

'And yet, so grand were her replies,
I could not choose but deem her wise;
I did not dare to criticise;

'Nor did I leave her, till she went
So deep in tangled argument
That all my powers of thought were spent.'

A little whisper inly slid;
'Yet truth is truth: you know you did –'
A little wink beneath the lid.

And, sickened with excess of dread,
Prone to the dust he bent his head,
And lay like one three-quarters dead.

Forth went the whisper like a breeze;
Left him amid the wondering trees,
Left him by no means at his ease.

Once more he weltered in despair,
With hands, through denser-matted hair,
More tightly clenched than then they were.

When, bathed in dawn of living red,
Majestic frowned the mountain head,
'Tell me my fault,' was all he said.

When, at high noon, the blazing sky
Scorched in his head each haggard eye,
Then keenest rose his weary cry.

And when at eve the unpitying sun
Smiled grimly on the solemn fun,
'Alack,' he sighed, 'what *have* I done?'

But saddest, darkest was the sight,
When the cold grasp of leaden Night
Dashed him to earth and held him tight.

Tortured, unaided, and alone,
Thunders were silence to his groan,
Bagpipes sweet music to its tone:

'What? Ever thus, in dismal round,
Shall Pain and Misery profound
Pursue me like a sleepless hound,

'With crimson-dashed and eager jaws,
Me, still in ignorance of the cause,
Unknowing what I brake of laws?'

The whisper to his ear did seem
Like echoed flow of silent stream,
Or shadow of forgotten dream;

The whisper trembling in the wind:
'Her fate with thine was intertwined,'
So spake it in his inner mind;

'Each orbed on each a baleful star,
Each proved the other's blight and bar,
Each unto each were best, most far:

'Yea, each to each was worse than foe,
Thou, a scared dullard, gibbering low,
And she, an avalanche of woe.'

The Valley of the Shadow of Death

Hark, said the dying man, and sighed,
    To that complaining tone –
Like sprite condemned, each eventide,
    To walk the world alone:
At sunset, when the air is still,
I hear it creep from yonder hill;
It breathes upon me, dead and chill,
    A moment, and is gone.

My son, it minds me of a day
    Left half a life behind,
That I have prayed to put away
    For ever from my mind.
But bitter memory will not die:
It haunts my soul when none is nigh:
I hear its whisper in the sigh
    Of that complaining wind.

And now in death my soul is fain
    To tell the tale of fear
That hidden in my breast hath lain
    Through many a weary year:
Yet time would fail to utter all –
The evil spells that held me thrall,
And thrust my life from fall to fall,
    Thou needest not to hear.

The spells that bound me with a chain
    Sin's stern behests to do,
Till Pleasure's self, invoked in vain,

A heavy burden grew –
Till from my spirit's fevered eye,
A hunted thing, I seemed to fly
Through the dark woods that underlie
    Yon mountain-range of blue.

Deep in those woods I found a vale
    No sunlight visiteth,
Nor star, nor wandering moonbeam pale;
    Where never comes the breath
Of summer breeze – there in mine ear,
Even as I lingered half in fear,
I heard a whisper, cold and clear,
    'This is the gate of Death.

'O bitter is it to abide
    In weariness alway;
At dawn to sigh for eventide,
    At eventide for day.
Thy noon is passed: thy sun hath shone:
The brightness of thy day is gone –
What need to lag and linger on
    Till life be cold and grey?

'O well,' it said, 'beneath yon pool,
    In some still cavern deep,
The fevered brain might slumber cool,
    The eyes forget to weep:
Within that goblet's mystic rim
Are draughts of healing, stored for him
Whose heart is sick, whose sight is dim,
    Who prayeth but to sleep!'

The evening-breeze went moaning by
    Like mourner for the dead,
And stirred, with shrill complaining sigh,
    The tree-tops overhead –
My guardian angel seemed to stand
And mutely wave a warning hand –
With sudden terror all unmanned,
    I turned myself and fled!

A cottage-gate stood open wide:
    Soft fell the dying ray
On two fair children, side by side,
    That rested from their play –
Together bent the earnest head,
As ever and anon they read
From one dear Book: the words they said
    Come back to me to-day.

Like twin cascades on mountain-stair
    Together wandered down
The ripples of the golden hair,
    The ripples of the brown:
While, through the tangled silken haze,
Blue eyes looked forth in eager gaze,
More starlike than the gems that blaze
    About a monarch's crown.

My son, there comes to each an hour
    When sinks the spirit's pride –
When weary hands forget their power
    The strokes of death to guide:
In such a moment, warriors say,

A word the panic rout may stay,
A sudden charge redeem the day
    And turn the living tide.

I could not see, for blinding tears,
    The glories of the west:
A heavenly music filled mine ears,
    A heavenly peace my breast.
'Come unto Me, come unto Me –
All ye that labour, unto Me –
Ye heavy-laden, come to Me –
    And I will give you rest.'

The night drew onward: thin and blue
    The evening mists arise
To bathe the thirsty land in dew,
    As erst in Paradise –
While over silent field and town
The deep blue vault of heaven looked down;
Not, as of old, in angry frown,
    But bright with angels' eyes.

Blest day! Then first I heard the voice
    That since hath oft beguiled
These eyes from tears, and bid rejoice
    This heart with anguish wild –
Thy mother, boy, thou hast not known,
So soon she left me here to moan –
Left me to weep and watch, alone,
    Our one beloved child.

Though, parted from my aching sight,
    Like homeward-speeding dove,
She passed into the perfect light
    That floods the world above;
Yet our twin spirits, well I know —
Though one abide in pain below —
Love, as in summers long ago,
    And evermore shall love.

So with a glad and patient heart
    I move toward mine end:
The streams, that flow awhile apart,
    Shall both in ocean blend.
I dare not weep: I can but bless
The Love that pitied my distress,
And lent me, in life's wilderness,
    So sweet and true a friend.

But if there be — O if there be
    A truth in what they say,
That angel-forms we cannot see
    Go with us on our way;
Then surely she is with me here,
I dimly feel her spirit near —
The morning mists grow thin and clear,
    And Death brings in the Day.

Beatrice

In her eyes is the living light
    Of a wanderer to earth
From a far celestial height:
    Summers five are all the span –
    Summers five since Time began
To veil in mists of human night
    A shining angel-birth.

Does an angel look from her eyes?
    Will she suddenly spring away,
And soar to her home in the skies?
    Beatrice! Blessing and blessed to be!
    Beatrice! Still as I gaze on thee,
Visions of two sweet maids arise,
    Whose life was of yesterday:

Of a Beatrice pale and stern,
    With the lips of a dumb despair,
With the innocent eyes that yearn –
    Yearn for the young sweet hours of life,
    Far from sorrow and far from strife,
For the happy summers that never return,
    When the world seemed good and fair:

Of a Beatrice glorious, bright –
    Of a sainted, ethereal maid,
Whose blue eyes are deep fountains of light,
    Cheering the poet that broodeth apart,
    Filling with gladness his desolate heart,

Like the moon when she shines thro' a cloudless night
    On a world of silence and shade.

And the visions waver and faint,
    And the visions vanish away
That my fancy delighted to paint –
    She is here at my side, a living child,
    With the glowing cheek and the tresses wild,
Nor death-pale martyr, nor radiant saint,
    Yet stainless and bright as they.

For I think, if a grim wild beast
    Were to come from his charnel-cave,
From his jungle-home in the East –
    Stealthily creeping with bated breath,
    Stealthily creeping with eyes of death –
He would all forget his dream of the feast,
    And crouch at her feet a slave.

She would twine her hand in his mane,
    She would prattle in silvery tone,
Like the tinkle of summer rain –
    Questioning him with her laughing eyes,
    Questioning him with a glad surprise,
Till she caught from those fierce eyes again
    The love that lit her own.

And be sure, if a savage heart,
    In a mask of human guise,
Were to come on her here apart –
    Bound for a dark and deadly deed,
    Hurrying past with pitiless speed –

He would suddenly falter and guiltily start
    At the glance of her pure blue eyes.

Nay, be sure, if an angel fair,
    A bright seraph undefiled,
Were to stoop from the trackless air,
    Fain would she linger in glad amaze —
    Lovingly linger to ponder and gaze,
With a sister's love and a sister's care,
    On the happy, innocent child.

The Sailor's Wife

See! There are tears upon her face –
    Tears newly shed, and scarcely dried:
Close, in an agonised embrace,
    She clasps the infant at her side.

Peace dwells in those soft-lidded eyes,
    And parted lips that faintly smile –
Peace, the foretaste of Paradise,
    In heart too young for care or guile.

No peace the mother's features wear;
    But quivering lip, and knotted brow,
And broken mutterings, all declare
    The fearful dream that haunts her now.

The storm-wind, rushing through the sky,
    Wails from the depths of cloudy space;
Shrill, piercing as the seaman's cry
    When Death and he are face to face.

Familiar tones are in the gale;
    They ring upon her startled ear:
And quick and low she pants the tale
    That tells of agony and fear:

'Still that phantom-ship is nigh –
    With a vexed and life-like motion,
All beneath an angry sky,
    Rocking on an angry ocean.

'Round the straining mast and shrouds
    Throng the spirits of the storm;
Darkly seen through driving clouds,
    Bends each gaunt and ghastly form.

'See! The good ship yields at last!
    Dumbly yields, and fights no more;
Driving in the frantic blast,
    Headlong on the fatal shore.

'Hark! I hear her battered side,
    With a low and sullen shock,
Dashed amid the foaming tide
    Full upon a sunken rock.

'His face shines out against the sky,
    Like a ghost, so cold and white;
With a dead despairing eye
    Gazing through the gathered night.

'Is he watching, through the dark,
    Where a mocking ghostly hand
Points to yonder feeble spark
    Glimmering from the distant land?

'Sees he, in this hour of dread,
    Hearth and home and wife and child?
Loved ones who, in summers fled,
    Clung to him and wept and smiled?

'Reeling sinks the fated bark
    To her tomb beneath the wave;

Must he perish in the dark —
    Not a hand stretched out to save?

'See the spirits, how they crowd!
    Watching death with eyes that burn!
Waves rush in —' she shrieks aloud,
    Ere her waking sense return.

The storm is gone: the skies are clear:
    Hush'd is that bitter cry of pain:
The only sound that meets her ear
    The heaving of the sullen main.

Though heaviness endure the night,
    But joy shall come with break of day;
She shudders with a strange delight —
    The fearful dream is pass'd away.

She wakes; the grey dawn streaks the dark;
    With early songs the copses ring:
Far off she hears the watch-dog bark
    A joyful bark of welcoming!

Stanzas for Music

The morn was bright, the steeds were light,
    The wedding guests were gay;
Young Ellen stood within the wood
    And watched them pass away.
She scarcely saw the gallant train,
    The tear-drop dimmed her ee;
Unheard the maiden did complain
    Beneath the Willow tree.

'O Robin, thou didst love me well,
    Till on a bitter day
She came, the Lady Isabel,
    And stole my Love away.
My tears are vain, I live again
    In days that used to be,
When I could meet thy welcome feet
    Beneath the Willow tree.

'O Willow grey, I may not stay
    Till Spring renew thy leaf,
But I will hide myself away,
    And nurse a hopeless grief.
It shall not dim life's joy for him,
    My tears he shall not see;
While he is by, I'll come not nigh
    My weeping Willow tree.

'But when I die, O let me lie
    Beneath thy loving shade,
That he may loiter careless by

Where I am lowly laid.
And let the white white marble tell,
    If he should stoop to see,
"Here lies a maid that loved thee well,
    Beneath the Willow tree."'

Three Sunsets

He saw her once, and in the glance,
    A moment's glance of meeting eyes,
His heart stood still in sudden trance:
    He trembled with a sweet surprise –
All in the waning light she stood,
The star of perfect womanhood.

That summer-eve his heart was light,
    With lighter step he trod the ground,
And life was fairer in his sight,
    And music was in every sound;
He blessed the world where there could be
So beautiful a thing as she.

There once again, as evening fell
    And stars were peering overhead,
Two lovers met to bid farewell:
    The western sun gleamed faint and red,
Lost in a drift of purple cloud
That wrapped him like a funeral-shroud.

Long time the memory of that night –
    The hand that clasped, the lips that kissed,
The form that faded from his sight
    Slow sinking through the tearful mist –
In dreamy music seemed to roll
Through the dark chambers of his soul.

So after many years he came
    A wanderer from a distant shore;

The street, the house, were still the same,
But those he sought were there no more:
His burning words, his hopes and fears,
Unheeded fell on alien ears.

Only the children from their play
Would pause the mournful tale to hear,
Shrinking in half-alarm away,
Or, step by step, would venture near
To touch with timid curious hands
That strange wild man from other lands.

He sat beside the busy street,
There, where he last had seen her face;
And thronging memories, bitter-sweet,
Seemed yet to haunt the ancient place:
Her footfall ever floated near,
Her voice was ever in his ear.

He sometimes, as the daylight waned
And evening mists began to roll,
In half-soliloquy complained
Of that black shadow on his soul,
And blindly fanned, with cruel care,
The ashes of a vain despair.

The summer fled: the lonely man
Still lingered out the lessening days:
Still, as the night drew on, would scan
Each passing face with closer gaze –
Till, sick at heart, he turned away,
And sighed 'she will not come to-day.'

So by degrees his spirit bent
    To mock its own despairing cry,
In strange self-torture to invent
    New luxuries of agony,
And people all the vacant space
With visions of her perfect face:

Till for a moment she was nigh,
    He heard no step, but she was there;
As if an angel suddenly
    Were bodied from the viewless air,
And all her fine ethereal frame
Should fade as strangely as it came.

So, half in fancy's sunny trance,
    And half in misery's aching void,
With set and stony countenance
    His bitter being he enjoyed,
And thrust for ever from his mind
The happiness he could not find.

As when the wretch, in lonely room,
    To selfish death is madly hurled,
The glamour of that fatal fume
    Shuts out the wholesome living world –
So all his manhood's strength and pride
One sickly dream had swept aside.

Yea, brother, and we passed him there,
    But yesterday, in merry mood,
And marvelled at the lordly air
    That shamed his beggar's attitude,

Nor heeded that ourselves might be
Wretches as desperate as he;

Who let the dream of bliss denied
    Make havoc of our life and powers,
And pine, in solitary pride,
    For peace that never shall be ours,
Because we will not work and wait
In trustful patience for our fate.

And so it chanced once more that she
    Came by the old familiar spot;
The face he would have died to see
    Bent o'er him, and he knew it not;
Too rapt in selfish grief to hear,
Even when happiness was near.

And pity filled her gentle breast
    For him that would not stir nor speak;
The dying crimson of the west,
    That faintly tinged his haggard cheek,
Fell on her as she stood, and shed
A glory round the patient head.

Awake, awake! The moments fly;
    This awful tryst may be the last.
And see! The tear that dimmed her eye,
    Had fallen on him ere she passed –
She passed; the crimson paled to grey:
And hope departed with the day.

The heavy hours of night went by,
        And silence quickened into sound,
And light slid up the eastern, sky,
        And life began its daily round –
But life and light for him were fled:
His name was numbered with the dead.

Faces in the Fire

The night creeps onward, sad and slow:
In these red embers' dying glow
The forms of Fancy come and go.

An island-farm – broad seas of corn
Stirred by the wandering breath of morn –
The happy spot where I was born.

The picture fadeth in its place:
Amid the glow I seem to trace
The shifting semblance of a face.

'Tis now a little childish form –
Red lips for kisses pouted warm –
And elf-locks tangled in the storm.

'Tis now a grave and gentle maid,
At her own beauty half afraid,
Shrinking, and willing to be stayed.

Oh, time was young, and life was warm,
When first I saw that fairy form,
Her dark hair tossing in the storm;

And fast and free these pulses played,
When last I met that gentle maid –
When last her hand in mine was laid.

Those locks of jet are turned to grey,
And she is strange and far away
That might have been mine own to-day –

That might have been mine own, my dear,
Through many and many a happy year –
That might have sat beside me here.

Aye, changeless through the changing scene,
The ghostly whisper rings between,
The dark refrain of 'might have been.'

The race is o'er I might have run,
The deeds are past I might have done,
And sere the wreath I might have won.

Sunk is the last faint flickering blaze;
The vision of departed days
Is vanished even as I gaze.

The pictures with their ruddy light
Are changed to dust and ashes white,
And I am left alone with night.

Fame's Penny-Trumpet

(*Affectionately dedicated to all 'original researchers' who pant for 'endowment'.*)

Blow, blow your trumpets till they crack,
Ye little men of little souls!
And bid them huddle at your back –
Gold-sucking leeches, shoals on shoals!

Fill all the air with hungry wails –
'Reward us, ere we think or write!
Without your Gold mere Knowledge fails
To sate the swinish appetite!'

And, where great Plato paced serene,
Or Newton paused with wistful eye,
Rush to the chace with hoofs unclean
And Babel-clamour of the sty.

Be yours the pay: be theirs the praise:
We will not rob them of their due,
Nor vex the ghosts of other days
By naming them along with you.

They sought and found undying fame:
They toiled not for reward nor thanks:
Their cheeks are hot with honest shame
For you, the modern mountebanks!

Who preach of Justice – plead with tears
That Love and Mercy should abound –

While marking with complacent ears
The moaning of some tortured hound:

Who prate of Wisdom – nay, forbear,
Lest Wisdom turn on you in wrath,
Trampling, with heel that will not spare,
The vermin that beset her path!

Go, throng each other's drawing-rooms,
Ye idols of a petty clique:
Strut your brief hour in borrowed plumes,
And make your penny-trumpets squeak.

Deck your dull talk with pilfered shreds
Of learning from a nobler time,
And oil each other's little heads
With mutual Flattery's golden slime:

And when the topmost height ye gain,
And stand in Glory's ether clear,
And grasp the prize of all your pain –
So many hundred pounds a year –

Then let Fame's banner be unfurled!
Sing Paeans for a victory won!
Ye tapers, that would light the world,
And cast a shadow on the Sun –

Who still shall pour His rays sublime,
One crystal flood, from East to West,
When YE have burned your little time
And feebly flickered into rest!

Tèma con Variazìòni

I never loved a dear Gazelle –
    Nor anything that cost me much:
High prices profit those who sell,
    But why should I be fond of such?

To glad me with his soft black eye
    My son comes trotting home from school;
He's had a fight but can't tell why –
    He always was a little fool!

But, when he came to know me well,
    He kicked me out, her testy Sire:
And when I stained my hair, that Belle
    Might note the change, and thus admire

And love me, it was sure to dye
    A muddy green or staring blue:
Whilst one might trace, with half an eye,
    The still triumphant carrot through.

All in the Golden Afternoon

All in the golden afternoon
    Full leisurely we glide;
For both our oars, with little skill,
    By little arms are plied,
While little hands make vain pretence
    Our wanderings to guide.

Ah, cruel Three! In such an hour,
    Beneath such dreamy weather,
To beg a tale of breath too weak
    To stir the tiniest feather!
Yet what can one poor voice avail
    Against three tongues together?

Imperious Prima flashes forth
    Her edict to 'begin it' –
In gentler tones Secunda hopes
    'There will be nonsense in it!'
While Tertia interrupts the tale
    Not more than once a minute.

Anon, to sudden silence won,
    In fancy they pursue
The dream-child moving through a land
    Of wonders wild and new,
In friendly chat with bird or beast –
    And half believe it true.

And ever, as the story drained
    The wells of fancy dry,

And faintly strove that weary one
        To put the subject by,
'The rest next time –' 'It *is* next time!'
        The happy voices cry.

Thus grew the tale of Wonderland:
        Thus slowly, one by one,
Its quaint events were hammered out –
        And now the tale is done,
And home we steer, a merry crew,
        Beneath the setting sun.

Alice! a childish story take,
        And, with a gentle hand,
Lay it where Childhood's dreams are twined
        In Memory's mystic band,
Like pilgrim's withered wreath of flowers
        Plucked in a far-off land.

A Boat Beneath a Sunny Sky

A boat beneath a sunny sky,
Lingering onward dreamily
In an evening of July –

Children three that nestle near,
Eager eye and willing ear,
Pleased a simple tale to hear –

Long has paled that sunny sky:
Echoes fade and memories die:
Autumn frosts have slain July.

Still she haunts me, phantomwise,
Alice moving under skies
Never seen by waking eyes.

Children yet, the tale to hear,
Eager eye and willing ear,
Lovingly shall nestle near.

In a Wonderland they lie,
Dreaming as the days go by,
Dreaming as the summers die:

Ever drifting down the stream –
Lingering in the golden gleam –
Life, what is it but a dream?

Jabberwocky

'Twas brillig, and the slithy toves
    Did gyre and gimble in the wabe:
All mimsy were the borogoves,
    And the mome raths outgrabe.

'Beware the Jabberwock, my son!
    The jaws that bite, the claws that catch!
Beware the Jubjub bird, and shun
    The frumious Bandersnatch!'

He took his vorpal sword in hand;
    Long time the manxome foe he sought –
So rested he by the Tumtum tree
    And stood awhile in thought.

And, as in uffish thought he stood,
    The Jabberwock, with eyes of flame,
Came whiffling through the tulgey wood,
    And burbled as it came!

One, two! One, two! And through and through
    The vorpal blade went snicker-snack!
He left it dead, and with its head
    He went galumphing back.

'And hast thou slain the Jabberwock?
    Come to my arms, my beamish boy!
O frabjous day! Callooh! Callay!'
    He chortled in his joy.

'Twas brillig, and the slithy toves
    Did gyre and gimble in the wabe:
All mimsy were the borogoves,
    And the mome raths outgrabe.

The Mock Turtle's Song

'Will you walk a little faster?' said a whiting to a snail,
'There's a porpoise close behind us, and he's treading on
     my tail.
See how eagerly the lobsters and the turtles all advance!
They are waiting on the shingle – will you come and join
     the dance?
    Will you, won't you, will you, won't you, will you
    join the dance?
    Will you, won't you, will you, won't you, will you
    join the dance?

'You can really have no notion how delightful it will be,
When they take us up and throw us, with the lobsters,
     out to sea!'
But the snail replied 'Too far, too far!' and gave a look
     askance –
Said he thanked the whiting kindly, but he would not join
     the dance.
    Would not, could not, would not, could not, would
    not join the dance.
    Would not, could not, would not, could not, would
    not join the dance.

'What matters it how far we go?' his scaly friend replied.
'There is another shore, you know, upon the other side.
The further off from England the nearer is to France –
Then turn not pale, beloved snail, but come and join the
     dance.
    Will you, won't you, will you, won't you, won't
    you join the dance?

Will you, won't you, will you, won't you, won't
you join the dance?'

The Duchess's Lullaby

'Speak roughly to your little boy,
    And beat him when he sneezes:
He only does it to annoy,
    Because he knows it teases.'

CHORUS
(In which the cook and the baby joined): –
'Wow! wow! wow!'

'I speak severely to my boy,
    I beat him when he sneezes;
For he can thoroughly enjoy
    The pepper when he pleases!'

CHORUS
'Wow! wow! wow!'

Twinkle, Twinkle, Little Bat

Twinkle, twinkle, little bat!
How I wonder what you're at!

Up above the world you fly,
Like a tea tray in the sky.

The White Knight's Song

I'll tell thee everything I can:
    There's little to relate.
I saw an aged, aged man,
    A-sitting on a gate.
'Who are you, aged man?' I said.
    'And how is it you live?'
And his answer trickled through my head,
    Like water through a sieve.

He said, 'I look for butterflies
    That sleep among the wheat;
I make them into mutton-pies,
    And sell them in the street.
I sell them unto men,' he said,
    'Who sail on stormy seas;
And that's the way I get my bread –
    A trifle, if you please.'

But I was thinking of a plan
    To dye one's whiskers green,
And always use so large a fan
    That they could not be seen.
So, having no reply to give
    To what the old man said,
I cried, 'Come, tell me how you live!'
    And thumped him on the head.

His accents mild took up the tale:
    He said, 'I go my ways,
And when I find a mountain-rill,

I set it in a blaze;
And thence they make a stuff they call
        Rowland's Macassar-Oil —
Yet twopence-halfpenny is all
        They give me for my toil.'

But I was thinking of a way
        To feed oneself on batter,
And so go on from day to day
        Getting a little fatter.
I shook him well from side to side,
        Until his face was blue,
'Come, tell me how you live,' I cried,
        'And what it is you do!'

He said, 'I hunt for haddocks' eyes
        Among the heather bright,
And work them into waistcoat-buttons
        In the silent night.
And these I do not sell for gold
        Or coin of silvery shine,
But for a copper halfpenny,
        And that will purchase nine.

'I sometimes dig for buttered rolls,
        Or set limed twigs for crabs;
I sometimes search the grassy knolls
        For wheels of hansom-cabs.
And that's the way' (he gave a wink)
        'By which I get my wealth —
And very gladly will I drink
        Your Honour's noble health.'

I heard him then, for I had just
 Completed my design
To keep the Menai bridge from rust
 By boiling it in wine.
I thanked him much for telling me
 The way he got his wealth,
But chiefly for his wish that he
 Might drink my noble health.

And now, if e'er by chance I put
 My fingers into glue,
Or madly squeeze a right-hand foot
 Into a left-hand shoe,
Or if I drop upon my toe
 A very heavy weight,
I weep, for it reminds me so
Of that old man I used to know –
Whose look was mild, whose speech was slow,
Whose hair was whiter than the snow,
Whose face was very like a crow,
With eyes, like cinders, all aglow,
Who seemed distracted with his woe,
Who rocked his body to and fro,
And muttered mumblingly and low,
As if his mouth were full of dough,
Who snorted like a buffalo –
That summer evening long ago,
 A-sitting on a gate.

The Voice of the Lobster

'Tis the voice of the Lobster: I heard him declare
'You have baked me too brown, I must sugar my hair.'
As a duck with its eyelids, so he with his nose
Trims his belt and his buttons, and turns out his toes.

When the sands are all dry, he is gay as a lark,
And will talk in contemptuous tones of the Shark:
But, when the tide rises and sharks are around,
His voice has a timid and tremulous sound.'

I passed by his garden, and marked, with one eye,
How the Owl and the Panther were sharing a pie:
The panther took pie crust, and gravy, and meat,
While the Owl had the dish as its share of the treat.
When the pie was all finished, the Owl, as a boon,
Was kindly permitted to pocket the spoon:
While the Panther received knife and fork with a growl,
And concluded the banquet by [eating the owl.]

The White Rabbit's Evidence

They told me you had been to her,
    And mentioned me to him.
She gave me a good character,
    But said I could not swim.

He sent them word I had not gone.
    (We know it to be true):
If she should push the matter on,
    What would become of you?

I gave her one, they gave him two,
    You gave us three or more;
They all returned from him to you,
    Though they were mine before.

If I or she should chance to be
    Involved in this affair,
He trusts to you to set them free,
    Exactly as we were.

My notion was that you had been
    (Before she had this fit)
An obstacle that came between
    Him, and ourselves, and it.

Don't let him know she liked them best,
    For this must ever be
A secret, kept from all the rest,
    Between yourself and me.

The Walrus and the Carpenter

The sun was shining on the sea,
    Shining with all his might:
He did his very best to make
    The billows smooth and bright –
And this was odd, because it was
    The middle of the night.

The moon was shining sulkily,
    Because she thought the sun
Had got no business to be there
    After the day was done –
'It's very rude of him,' she said,
    'To come and spoil the fun.'

The sea was wet as wet could be,
    The sands were dry as dry.
You could not see a cloud, because
    No cloud was in the sky:
No birds were flying overhead –
    There were no birds to fly.

The Walrus and the Carpenter
    Were walking close at hand.
They wept like anything to see
    Such quantities of sand:
'If this were only cleared away,'
    They said, 'it would be grand!'

If seven maids with seven mops
    Swept it for half a year,

'Do you suppose,' the Walrus said,
    'That they could get it clear?'
'I doubt it,' said the Carpenter,
    And shed a bitter tear.

'O Oysters, come and walk with us!'
    The Walrus did beseech.
'A pleasant walk, a pleasant talk,
    Along the briny beach:
We cannot do with more than four,
    To give a hand to each.'

The eldest Oyster looked at him,
    But never a word he said:
The eldest Oyster winked his eye,
    And shook his heavy head –
Meaning to say he did not choose
    To leave the oyster-bed.

But four young Oysters hurried up,
    All eager for the treat:
Their coats were brushed, their faces washed,
    Their shoes were clean and neat –
And this was odd, because, you know,
    They hadn't any feet.

Four other Oysters followed them,
    And yet another four;
And thick and fast they came at last,
    And more, and more, and more –
All hopping through the frothy waves,

And scrambling to the shore.
The Walrus and the Carpenter
  Walked on a mile or so,
And then they rested on a rock
  Conveniently low:
And all the little Oysters stood
  And waited in a row.

'The time has come,' the Walrus said,
  'To talk of many things:
Of shoes – and ships – and sealing-wax –
  Of cabbages – and kings –
And why the sea is boiling hot –
  And whether pigs have wings.'

'But wait a bit,' the Oysters cried,
  'Before we have our chat;
For some of us are out of breath,
  And all of us are fat!'
'No hurry!' said the Carpenter.
  They thanked him much for that.

'A loaf of bread,' the Walrus said,
  'Is what we chiefly need:
Pepper and vinegar besides
  Are very good indeed –
Now if you're ready, Oysters dear,
  We can begin to feed.'

'But not on us!' the Oysters cried,
  Turning a little blue.
'After such kindness, that would be

A dismal thing to do!'
'The night is fine,' the Walrus said.
   'Do you admire the view?

'It was so kind of you to come!
   And you are very nice!'
The Carpenter said nothing but
   'Cut us another slice,
I wish you were not quite so deaf –
   I've had to ask you twice!'

'It seems a shame,' the Walrus said,
   'To play them such a trick,
After we've brought them out so far,
   And made them trot so quick!'
The Carpenter said nothing but
   'The butter's spread too thick!'

'I weep for you,' the Walrus said:
   'I deeply sympathise.'
With sobs and tears he sorted out
   Those of the largest size,
Holding his pocket-handkerchief
   Before his streaming eyes.

'O Oysters,' said the Carpenter,
   'You've had a pleasant run!
Shall we be trotting home again?'
   But answer came there none –
And this was scarcely odd, because
   They'd eaten every one.

You are old, Father William

'You are old, Father William,' the young man said,
　　'And your hair has become very white;
And yet you incessantly stand on your head –
　　Do you think, at your age, it is right?'

'In my youth,' Father William replied to his son,
　　'I feared it might injure the brain;
But, now that I'm perfectly sure I have none,
　　Why, I do it again and again.'

'You are old,' said the youth, 'as I mentioned before,
　　And you have grown must uncommonly fat;
Yet you turned a back-somersault in at the door –
　　Pray, what is the reason of that?'

'In my youth,' said the sage, as he shook his grey locks,
　　'I kept all my limbs very supple
By the use of this ointment – one shilling a box –
　　Allow me to sell you a couple?'

'You are old,' said the youth, 'and your jaws are too weak
　　For anything tougher than suet;
Yet you finished the goose, with the bones and the beak –
　　Pray, how did you manage to do it?'

'In my youth,' said his father, 'I took to the law,
　　And argued each case with my wife;
And the muscular strength, which it gave to my jaw
　　Has lasted the rest of my life.'

'You are old,' said the youth, 'one would hardly suppose
        That your eyes was as steady as ever;
Yet you balanced an eel on the end of your nose –
        What made you so awfully clever?'

'I have answered three questions, and that is enough,'
        Said his father. 'Don't give yourself airs!
Do you think I can listen all day to such stuff?
        Be off, or I'll kick you downstairs!'

Double Acrostic

Thanks, thanks, fair Cousins, for your gift
    So swiftly borne to Albion's isle –
Though angry waves their crests uplift
    Between our shores, for many a league!

('So far, so good,' you say: 'but how
    Your Cousins?' Let me tell you, Madam.
We're both descended, you'll allow,
    From one great-great-great-grandsire, Noah.)

Your picture shall adorn the book
    That's bound, so neatly and moroccoly,
With that bright green which every cook
    Delights to see in beds of cauliflower.

The carte is very good, but pray
    Send me the larger one as well!
'A cool request!' I hear you say.
    'Give him an inch, he takes an acre!'

'But we'll be generous because
    We well remember, in the story,
How good and gentle Alice was,
    The day she argued with the Parrot!'

The Hunting of the Snark

Fit the First
The Landing

'Just the place for a Snark!' the Bellman cried,
  As he landed his crew with care;
Supporting each man on the top of the tide
  By a finger entwined in his hair.

'Just the place for a Snark! I have said it twice:
  That alone should encourage the crew.
Just the place for a Snark! I have said it thrice:
  What I tell you three times is true.'

The crew was complete: it included a Boots –
  A maker of Bonnets and Hoods –
A Barrister, brought to arrange their disputes –
  And a Broker, to value their goods.

A Billiard-marker, whose skill was immense,
  Might perhaps have won more than his share –
But a Banker, engaged at enormous expense,
  Had the whole of their cash in his care.

There was also a Beaver, that paced on the deck,
  Or would sit making lace in the bow:
And had often (the Bellman said) saved them from wreck,
  Though none of the sailors knew how.

There was one who was famed for the number of things
  He forgot when he entered the ship:

His umbrella, his watch, all his jewels and rings,
  And the clothes he had bought for the trip.

He had forty-two boxes, all carefully packed,
  With his name painted clearly on each:
But, since he omitted to mention the fact,
  They were all left behind on the beach.

The loss of his clothes hardly mattered, because
  He had seven coats on when he came,
With three pair of boots – but the worst of it was,
  He had wholly forgotten his name.

He would answer to 'Hi!' or to any loud cry,
  Such as 'Fry me!' or 'Fritter my wig!'
To 'What-you-may-call-um!' or 'What-was-his-name!'
  But especially 'Thing-um-a-jig!'

While, for those who preferred a more forcible word,
  He had different names from these:
His intimate friends called him 'Candle-ends,'
  And his enemies 'Toasted-cheese.'

'His form is ungainly – his intellect small –'
  (So the Bellman would often remark) –
'But his courage is perfect! And that, after all,
  Is the thing that one needs with a Snark.'

He would joke with hyaenas, returning their stare
  With an impudent wag of the head:
And he once went a walk, paw-in-paw, with a bear,
  'Just to keep up its spirits,' he said.

He came as a Baker: but owned, when too late –
    And it drove the poor Bellman half-mad –
He could only bake Bride cake – for which, I may state,
    No materials were to be had.

The last of the crew needs especial remark,
    Though he looked an incredible dunce:
He had just one idea – but, that one being 'Snark,'
    The good Bellman engaged him at once.

He came as a Butcher: but gravely declared,
    When the ship had been sailing a week,
He could only kill Beavers. The Bellman looked scared,
    And was almost too frightened to speak:

But at length he explained, in a tremulous tone,
    There was only one Beaver on board;
And that was a tame one he had of his own,
    Whose death would be deeply deplored.

The Beaver, who happened to hear the remark,
    Protested, with tears in its eyes,
That not even the rapture of hunting the Snark
    Could atone for that dismal surprise!

It strongly advised that the Butcher should be
    Conveyed in a separate ship:
But the Bellman declared that would never agree
    With the plans he had made for the trip:

Navigation was always a difficult art,
    Though with only one ship and one bell:

And he feared he must really decline, for his part,
    Undertaking another as well.

The Beaver's best course was, no doubt, to procure
    A second-hand dagger-proof coat –
So the Baker advised it – and next, to insure
    Its life in some Office of note:

This the Banker suggested, and offered for hire
    (On moderate terms), or for sale,
Two excellent Policies, one Against Fire,
    And one Against Damage From Hail.

Yet still, ever after that sorrowful day,
    Whenever the Butcher was by,
The Beaver kept looking the opposite way,
    And appeared unaccountably shy.

Fit the Second
The Bellman's Speech

The Bellman himself they all praised to the skies –
    Such a carriage, such ease and such grace!
Such solemnity, too! One could see he was wise,
    The moment one looked in his face!

He had bought a large map representing the sea,
    Without the least vestige of land:
And the crew were much pleased when they found it to be
    A map they could all understand.

'What's the good of Mercator's North Poles and Equators,
        Tropics, Zones, and Meridian Lines?'
So the Bellman would cry: and the crew would reply
        'They are merely conventional signs!

'Other maps are such shapes, with their islands and capes!
        But we've got our brave Captain to thank'
(So the crew would protest) 'that he's bought us the best –
        A perfect and absolute blank!'

This was charming, no doubt; but they shortly found out
        That the Captain they trusted so well
Had only one notion for crossing the ocean,
        And that was to tingle his bell.

He was thoughtful and grave – but the orders he gave
        Were enough to bewilder a crew.
When he cried 'Steer to starboard, but keep her head larboard!'
        What on earth was the helmsman to do?

Then the bowsprit got mixed with the rudder sometimes:
        A thing, as the Bellman remarked,
That frequently happens in tropical climes,
        When a vessel is, so to speak, 'snarked.'

But the principal failing occurred in the sailing,
        And the Bellman, perplexed and distressed,
Said he had hoped, at least, when the wind blew due East,
        That the ship would not travel due West!

But the danger was past – they had landed at last,
        With their boxes, portmanteaus, and bags:

Yet at first sight the crew were not pleased with the view,
    Which consisted to chasms and crags.

The Bellman perceived that their spirits were low,
    And repeated in musical tone
Some jokes he had kept for a season of woe –
    But the crew would do nothing but groan.

He served out some grog with a liberal hand,
    And bade them sit down on the beach:
And they could not but own that their Captain looked
    grand,
    As he stood and delivered his speech.

'Friends, Romans, and countrymen, lend me your ears!'
    (They were all of them fond of quotations:
So they drank to his health, and they gave him three cheers,
    While he served out additional rations).

'We have sailed many months, we have sailed many weeks,
    (Four weeks to the month you may mark),
But never as yet ('tis your Captain who speaks)
    Have we caught the least glimpse of a Snark!

'We have sailed many weeks, we have sailed many days,
    (Seven days to the week I allow),
But a Snark, on the which we might lovingly gaze,
    We have never beheld till now!

'Come, listen, my men, while I tell you again
    The five unmistakable marks

By which you may know, wheresoever you go,
    The warranted genuine Snarks.

'Let us take them in order. The first is the taste,
    Which is meagre and hollow, but crisp:
Like a coat that is rather too tight in the waist,
    With a flavour of Will-o'-the-wisp.

'Its habit of getting up late you'll agree
    That it carries too far, when I say
That it frequently breakfasts at five-o'clock tea,
    And dines on the following day.

'The third is its slowness in taking a jest.
    Should you happen to venture on one,
It will sigh like a thing that is deeply distressed:
    And it always looks grave at a pun.

'The fourth is its fondness for bathing-machines,
    Which it constantly carries about,
And believes that they add to the beauty of scenes –
    A sentiment open to doubt.

'The fifth is ambition. It next will be right
    To describe each particular batch:
Distinguishing those that have feathers, and bite,
    From those that have whiskers, and scratch.

'For, although common Snarks do no manner of harm,
    Yet, I feel it my duty to say,
Some are Boojums –' The Bellman broke off in alarm,
    For the Baker had fainted away.

Fit the Third
The Baker's Tale

They roused him with muffins – they roused him with ice –
    They roused him with mustard and cress –
They roused him with jam and judicious advice –
    They set him conundrums to guess.

When at length he sat up and was able to speak,
    His sad story he offered to tell;
And the Bellman cried 'Silence! Not even a shriek!'
    And excitedly tingled his bell.

There was silence supreme! Not a shriek, not a scream,
    Scarcely even a howl or a groan,
As the man they called 'Ho!' told his story of woe
    In an antediluvian tone.

'My father and mother were honest, though poor –'
    'Skip all that!' cried the Bellman in haste.
'If it once becomes dark, there's no chance of a Snark –
    We have hardly a minute to waste!

'I skip forty years,' said the Baker, in tears,
    'And proceed without further remark
To the day when you took me aboard of your ship
    To help you in hunting the Snark.

'A dear uncle of mine (after whom I was named)
    Remarked, when I bade him farewell –'

'Oh, skip your dear uncle!' the Bellman exclaimed,
    As he angrily tingled his bell.

'He remarked to me then,' said that mildest of men,
    '"If your Snark be a Snark, that is right:
Fetch it home by all means – you may serve it with greens,
    And it's handy for striking a light.

'"You may seek it with thimbles – and seek it with care;
    You may hunt it with forks and hope;
You may threaten its life with a railway-share;
    You may charm it with smiles and soap –"'

('That's exactly the method,' the Bellman bold
    In a hasty parenthesis cried,
'That's exactly the way I have always been told
    That the capture of Snarks should be tried!')

'"But oh, beamish nephew, beware of the day,
    If your Snark be a Boojum! For then
You will softly and suddenly vanish away,
    And never be met with again!"

'It is this, it is this that oppresses my soul,
    When I think of my uncle's last words:
And my heart is like nothing so much as a bowl
    Brimming over with quivering curds!

'It is this, it is this –' 'We have had that before!'
    The Bellman indignantly said.

And the Baker replied 'Let me say it once more.
　　　　It is this, it is this that I dread!

'I engage with the Snark — every night after dark —
　　　　In a dreamy delirious fight:
I serve it with greens in those shadowy scenes,
　　　　And I use it for striking a light:

'But if ever I meet with a Boojum, that day,
　　　　In a moment (of this I am sure),
I shall softly and suddenly vanish away —
　　　　And the notion I cannot endure!'

Fit the Fourth
The Hunting

The Bellman looked uffish, and wrinkled his brow.
　　　　'If only you'd spoken before!
It's excessively awkward to mention it now,
　　　　With the Snark, so to speak, at the door!

'We should all of us grieve, as you well may believe,
　　　　If you never were met with again —
But surely, my man, when the voyage began,
　　　　You might have suggested it then?

'It's excessively awkward to mention it now —
　　　　As I think I've already remarked.'
And the man they called 'Hi!' replied, with a sigh,
　　　　'I informed you the day we embarked.

'You may charge me with murder – or want of sense –
        (We are all of us weak at times):
But the slightest approach to a false pretence
        Was never among my crimes!

'I said it in Hebrew – I said it in Dutch –
        I said it in German and Greek:
But I wholly forgot (and it vexes me much)
        That English is what you speak!'

''Tis a pitiful tale,' said the Bellman, whose face
        Had grown longer at every word:
'But, now that you've stated the whole of your case,
        More debate would be simply absurd.

'The rest of my speech' (he explained to his men)
        'You shall hear when I've leisure to speak it.
But the Snark is at hand, let me tell you again!
        'Tis your glorious duty to seek it!

'To seek it with thimbles, to seek it with care;
        To pursue it with forks and hope;
To threaten its life with a railway-share;
        To charm it with smiles and soap!

'For the Snark's a peculiar creature, that won't
        Be caught in a commonplace way.
Do all that you know, and try all that you don't:
        Not a chance must be wasted to-day!

'For England expects – I forbear to proceed:
        'Tis a maxim tremendous, but trite:

And you'd best be unpacking the things that you need
       To rig yourselves out for the fight.'

Then the Banker endorsed a blank check (which he crossed),
       And changed his loose silver for notes.
The Baker with care combed his whiskers and hair,
       And shook the dust out of his coats:

The Boots and the Broker were sharpening a spade –
       Each working the grindstone in turn:
But the Beaver went on making lace, and displayed
       No interest in the concern:

Though the Barrister tried to appeal to its pride,
       And vainly proceeded to cite
A number of cases, in which making laces
       Had been proved an infringement of right.

The maker of Bonnets ferociously planned
       A novel arrangement of bows:
While the Billiard-marker with quivering hand
       Was chalking the tip of his nose.

But the Butcher turned nervous, and dressed himself fine,
       With yellow kid gloves and a ruff –
Said he felt it exactly like going to dine,
       Which the Bellman declared was all 'stuff.'

'Introduce me, now there's a good fellow,' he said,
       'If we happen to meet it together!'
And the Bellman, sagaciously nodding his head,
       Said 'That must depend on the weather.'

The Beaver went simply galumphing about,
     At seeing the Butcher so shy:
And even the Baker, though stupid and stout,
     Made an effort to wink with one eye.

'Be a man!' said the Bellman in wrath, as he heard
     The Butcher beginning to sob.
'Should we meet with a Jubjub, that desperate bird,
     We shall need all our strength for the job!'

Fit the Fifth
The Beaver's Lesson

They sought it with thimbles, they sought it with care;
     They pursued it with forks and hope;
They threatened its life with a railway-share;
     They charmed it with smiles and soap.

Then the Butcher contrived an ingenious plan
     For making a separate sally;
And had fixed on a spot unfrequented by man,
     A dismal and desolate valley.

But the very same plan to the Beaver occurred:
     It had chosen the very same place:
Yet neither betrayed, by a sign or a word,
     The disgust that appeared in his face.

Each thought he was thinking of nothing but 'Snark'
     And the glorious work of the day;
And each tried to pretend that he did not remark
     That the other was going that way.

But the valley grew narrow and narrower still,
　　And the evening got darker and colder,
Till (merely from nervousness, not from goodwill)
　　They marched along shoulder to shoulder.

Then a scream, shrill and high, rent the shuddering sky,
　　And they knew that some danger was near:
The Beaver turned pale to the tip of its tail,
　　And even the Butcher felt queer.

He thought of his childhood, left far far behind –
　　That blissful and innocent state –
The sound so exactly recalled to his mind
　　A pencil that squeaks on a slate!

''Tis the voice of the Jubjub!' he suddenly cried.
　　(This man, that they used to call 'Dunce.')
'As the Bellman would tell you,' he added with pride,
　　'I have uttered that sentiment once.

''Tis the note of the Jubjub! Keep count, I entreat.
　　You will find I have told it you twice.
'Tis the song of the Jubjub! The proof is complete,
　　If only I've stated it thrice.'

The Beaver had counted with scrupulous care,
　　Attending to every word:
But it fairly lost heart, and outgrabe in despair,
　　When the third repetition occurred.

It felt that, in spite of all possible pains,
　　It had somehow contrived to lose count,

And the only thing now was to rack its poor brains
    By reckoning up the amount.

'Two added to one – if that could but be done,'
    It said, 'with one's fingers and thumbs!'
Recollecting with tears how, in earlier years,
    It had taken no pains with its sums.

'The thing can be done,' said the Butcher, 'I think.
    The thing must be done, I am sure.
The thing shall be done! Bring me paper and ink,
    The best there is time to procure.'

The Beaver brought paper, portfolio, pens,
    And ink in unfailing supplies:
While strange creepy creatures came out of their dens,
    And watched them with wondering eyes.

So engrossed was the Butcher, he heeded them not,
    As he wrote with a pen in each hand,
And explained all the while in a popular style
    Which the Beaver could well understand.

'Taking Three as the subject to reason about –
    A convenient number to state –
We add Seven, and Ten, and then multiply out
    By One Thousand diminished by Eight.

'The result we proceed to divide, as you see,
    By Nine Hundred and Ninety and Two:
Then subtract Seventeen, and the answer must be
    Exactly and perfectly true.

'The method employed I would gladly explain,
      While I have it so clear in my head,
If I had but the time and you had but the brain –
      But much yet remains to be said.

'In one moment I've seen what has hitherto been
      Enveloped in absolute mystery,
And without extra charge I will give you at large
      A Lesson in Natural History.'

In his genial way he proceeded to say
      (Forgetting all laws of propriety,
And that giving instruction, without introduction,
      Would have caused quite a thrill in Society),

'As to temper the Jubjub's a desperate bird,
      Since it lives in perpetual passion:
Its taste in costume is entirely absurd –
      It is ages ahead of the fashion:

'But it knows any friend it has met once before:
      It never will look at a bribe:
And in charity-meetings it stands at the door,
      And collects – though it does not subscribe.

'Its flavour when cooked is more exquisite far
      Than mutton, or oysters, or eggs:
(Some think it keeps best in an ivory jar,
      And some, in mahogany kegs:)

'You boil it in sawdust: you salt it in glue:
  You condense it with locusts and tape:
Still keeping one principal object in view –
  To preserve its symmetrical shape.'

The Butcher would gladly have talked till next day,
  But he felt that the lesson must end,
And he wept with delight in attempting to say
  He considered the Beaver his friend:

While the Beaver confessed, with affectionate looks
  More eloquent even than tears,
It had learned in ten minutes far more than all books
  Would have taught it in seventy years.

They returned hand-in-hand, and the Bellman, unmanned
  (For a moment) with noble emotion,
Said 'This amply repays all the wearisome days
  We have spent on the billowy ocean!'

Such friends, as the Beaver and Butcher became,
  Have seldom if ever been known;
In winter or summer, 'twas always the same –
  You could never meet either alone.

And when quarrels arose – as one frequently finds
  Quarrels will, spite of every endeavour –
The song of the Jubjub recurred to their minds,
  And cemented their friendship for ever!

Fit the Sixth
The Barrister's Dream

They sought it with thimbles, they sought it with care;
　　They pursued it with forks and hope;
They threatened its life with a railway-share;
　　They charmed it with smiles and soap.

But the Barrister, weary of proving in vain
　　That the Beaver's lace-making was wrong,
Fell asleep, and in dreams saw the creature quite plain
　　That his fancy had dwelt on so long.

He dreamed that he stood in a shadowy Court,
　　Where the Snark, with a glass in its eye,
Dressed in gown, bands, and wig, was defending a pig
　　On the charge of deserting its sty.

The Witnesses proved, without error or flaw,
　　That the sty was deserted when found:
And the Judge kept explaining the state of the law
　　In a soft under-current of sound.

The indictment had never been clearly expressed,
　　And it seemed that the Snark had begun,
And had spoken three hours, before any one guessed
　　What the pig was supposed to have done.

The Jury had each formed a different view
　　(Long before the indictment was read),
And they all spoke at once, so that none of them knew
　　One word that the others had said.

'You must know –' said the Judge: but the Snark
   exclaimed 'Fudge!'
      That statute is obsolete quite!
Let me tell you, my friends, the whole question depends
      On an ancient manorial right.

'In the matter of Treason the pig would appear
      To have aided, but scarcely abetted:
While the charge of Insolvency fails, it is clear,
      If you grant the plea "never indebted."

'The fact of Desertion I will not dispute;
      But its guilt, as I trust, is removed
(So far as relates to the costs of this suit)
      By the Alibi which has been proved.

'My poor client's fate now depends on your votes.'
      Here the speaker sat down in his place,
And directed the Judge to refer to his notes
      And briefly to sum up the case.

But the Judge said he never had summed up before;
      So the Snark undertook it instead,
And summed it so well that it came to far more
      Than the Witnesses ever had said!

When the verdict was called for, the Jury declined,
      As the word was so puzzling to spell;
But they ventured to hope that the Snark wouldn't mind
Undertaking that duty as well.

So the Snark found the verdict, although, as it owned,
     It was spent with the toils of the day:
When it said the word 'GUILTY!' the Jury all groaned,
     And some of them fainted away.

Then the Snark pronounced sentence, the Judge being quite
     Too nervous to utter a word:
When it rose to its feet, there was silence like night,
     And the fall of a pin might be heard.

'Transportation for life' was the sentence it gave,
     'And then to be fined forty pound.'
The Jury all cheered, though the Judge said he feared
     That the phrase was not legally sound.

But their wild exultation was suddenly checked
     When the jailer informed them, with tears,
Such a sentence would have not the slightest effect,
     As the pig had been dead for some years.

The Judge left the Court, looking deeply disgusted:
     But the Snark, though a little aghast,
As the lawyer to whom the defence was intrusted,
     Went bellowing on to the last.

Thus the Barrister dreamed, while the bellowing seemed
     To grow every moment more clear:
Till he woke to the knell of a furious bell,
     Which the Bellman rang close at his ear.

Fit the Seventh

The Banker's Fate

They sought it with thimbles, they sought it with care;
 They pursued it with forks and hope;
They threatened its life with a railway-share;
 They charmed it with smiles and soap.

And the Banker, inspired with a courage so new
 It was matter for general remark,
Rushed madly ahead and was lost to their view
 In his zeal to discover the Snark.

But while he was seeking with thimbles and care,
 A Bandersnatch swiftly drew nigh
And grabbed at the Banker, who shrieked in despair,
 For he knew it was useless to fly.

He offered large discount – he offered a cheque
 (Drawn 'to bearer') for seven-pounds-ten:
But the Bandersnatch merely extended its neck
 And grabbed at the Banker again.

Without rest or pause – while those frumious jaws
 Went savagely snapping around –
He skipped and he hopped, and he floundered and flopped,
 Till fainting he fell to the ground.

The Bandersnatch fled as the others appeared
 Led on by that fear-stricken yell:
And the Bellman remarked 'It is just as I feared!'
 And solemnly tolled on his bell.

He was black in the face, and they scarcely could trace
        The least likeness to what he had been:
While so great was his fright that his waistcoat turned white –
        A wonderful thing to be seen!

To the horror of all who were present that day,
        He uprose in full evening dress,
And with senseless grimaces endeavoured to say
        What his tongue could no longer express.

Down he sank in a chair – ran his hands through his hair –
        And chanted in mimsiest tones
Words whose utter inanity proved his insanity,
        While he rattled a couple of bones.

'Leave him here to his fate – it is getting so late!'
        The Bellman exclaimed in a fright.
'We have lost half the day. Any further delay,
        And we sha'n't catch a Snark before night!'

Fit the Eighth
The Vanishing

They sought it with thimbles, they sought it with care;
        They pursued it with forks and hope;
They threatened its life with a railway-share;
        They charmed it with smiles and soap.

They shuddered to think that the chase might fail,
        And the Beaver, excited at last,
Went bounding along on the tip of its tail,
        For the daylight was nearly past.

'There is Thingumbob shouting!' the Bellman said,
    'He is shouting like mad, only hark!
He is waving his hands, he is wagging his head,
    He has certainly found a Snark!'

They gazed in delight, while the Butcher exclaimed
    'He was always a desperate wag!'
They beheld him – their Baker – their hero unnamed –
    On the top of a neighbouring crag,

Erect and sublime, for one moment of time,
    In the next, that wild figure they saw
(As if stung by a spasm) plunge into a chasm,
    While they waited and listened in awe.

'It's a Snark!' was the sound that first came to their ears,
    And seemed almost too good to be true.
Then followed a torrent of laughter and cheers:
    Then the ominous words 'It's a Boo—'

Then, silence. Some fancied they heard in the air
    A weary and wandering sigh
That sounded like '—jum!' but the others declare
    It was only a breeze that went by.

They hunted till darkness came on, but they found
    Not a button, or feather, or mark,
By which they could tell that they stood on the ground
    Where the Baker had met with the Snark.

In the midst of the word he was trying to say,
    In the midst of his laughter and glee,

He had softly and suddenly vanished away –
For the Snark *was* a Boojum, you see.

Size and Tears

When on the sandy shore I sit,
    Beside the salt sea-wave,
And fall into a weeping fit
    Because I dare not shave –
A little whisper at my ear
Enquires the reason of my fear.

I answer 'If that ruffian Jones,
    Should recognise me here,
He'd bellow out my name in tones
    Offensive to the ear:
He chaffs me so on being stout
(A thing that always puts me out).'

Ah me! I see him on the cliff!
    Farewell, farewell to hope,
If he should look this way, and if
    He's got his telescope!
To whatsoever place I flee,
My odious rival follows me!

For every night, and everywhere,
    I meet him out at dinner;
And when I've found some charming fair,
    And vowed to die or win her,
The wretch (he's thin and I am stout)
Is sure to come and cut me out!

The girls (just like them!) all agree
    To praise J. Jones, Esquire:

I ask them what on earth they see
     About him to admire?
They cry 'He is so sleek and slim,
It's quite a treat to look at him!'

They vanish in tobacco smoke,
     Those visionary maids –
I feel a sharp and sudden poke
     Between the shoulder-blades –
'Why, Brown, my boy! Your growing stout!'
(I told you he would find me out!)

'My growth is not your business, Sir!'
     'No more it is, my boy!
But if it's yours, as I infer,
     Why, Brown, I give you joy!'
A man, whose business prospers so,
Is just the sort of man to know!

'It's hardly safe, though, talking here –
     I'd best get out of reach:
For such a weight as yours, I fear,
     Must shortly sink the beach!' –
Insult me thus because I'm stout!
I vow I'll go and call him out!

Another Acrostic

(In the style of *Father William*)

'Are you deaf, Father William?' the young man said,
'Did you hear what I told you just now?
Excuse me for shouting! Don't waggle your head
Like a blundering, sleepy old cow!

'A little maid dwelling in Wallington Town,
Is my friend, so I beg to remark:
Do you think she'd be pleased if a book were sent down
Entitled "The Hunt of the Snark?"'

'Pack it up in brown paper!' the old man cried,
'And seal it with olive-and-dove.
I command you to do it!' he added with pride,
'Nor forget, my good fellow to send her beside
Easter Greetings, and give her my love.'

Madrigal

(To Miss May Forshall)

He shouts amain, he shouts again,
    (Her brother, fierce, as bluff King Hal),
'I tell you flat, I shall do that!'
    She softly whispers '"May" for "shall"!'

He wistful sighed one eventide
    (Her friend, that made this Madrigal),
'And shall I kiss you, pretty Miss!'
    She softly whispers '"May" for "shall"!'

With eager eyes my reader cries,
    'Your friend must be indeed a val-
-uable child, so sweet, so mild!
    What do you call her?' 'May For shall.'

Echoes

Lady Clara Vere de Vere
Was eight years old, she said:
Every ringlet, lightly shaken, ran itself in golden thread

She took her little porringer:
Of me she shall not win renown:
For the baseness of its nature shall have strength to
    drag her down.

'Sisters and brothers, little Maid?
There stands the Inspector at thy door:
Like a dog, he hunts for boys who know not two and
    two are four.'

'Kind words are more than coronets,'
She said, and wondering looked at me:
'It is the dead unhappy night, and I must hurry home to tea.'

Christmas Greetings

(*From a Fairy to a Child.*)

Lady dear, if fairies may,
    For a moment lay aside
Cunning tricks and elfish play –
    'Tis at happy Christmas-tide.

We have heard the children say –
    Gentle children, whom we love –
Long ago, on Christmas Day,
    Came a message from above.

Still, as Christmas-tide comes round,
    They remember it again –
Echo still the joyful sound,
    'Peace on earth, good will to men!'

Yet the hearts must child-like be
    Where such heavenly guests abide:
Unto children, in their glee
    All the year is Christmas-tide!

Thus, forgetting tricks and play
    For a moment, lady dear,
We would wish you, if we may,
    Merry Christmas, glad New Year!

A Nursery Darling

A Mother's breast:
Safe refuge from her childish fears,
From childish troubles, childish tears,
Mists that enshroud her dawning years!
See how in sleep she seems to sing
A voiceless psalm – an offering
Raised, to the glory of her King
In Love: for Love is Rest.

A Darling's kiss:
Dearest of all the signs that fleet
From lips that lovingly repeat
Again, again, the message sweet!
Full to the brim with girlish glee,
A child, a very child is she,
Whose dream of Heaven is still to be
At Home: for Home is Bliss.

Little Birds

Little Birds are dining
    Warily and well,
    Hid in mossy cell:
Hid, I say, by waiters
Gorgeous in their gaiters –
    I've a Tale to tell.

Little Birds are feeding
    Justices with jam,
    Rich in frizzled ham:
Rich, I say, in oysters
Haunting shady cloisters –
    That is what I am.

Little Birds are teaching
    Tigresses to smile,
    Innocent of guile:
Smile, I say, not smirkle –
Mouth a semicircle,
    That's the proper style!

Little Birds are sleeping
    All among the pins,
    Where the loser wins:
Where, I say, he sneezes
When and how he pleases –
    So the Tale begins.

Little Birds are writing
    Interesting books,

To be read by cooks:
Read, I say, not roasted –
Letterpress, when toasted,
        Loses its good looks.

Little Birds are playing
        Bagpipes on the shore,
        Where the tourists snore:
'Thanks!' they cry. ''Tis thrilling!
Take, oh take this shilling!
        Let us have no more!'

Little Birds are bathing
        Crocodiles in cream,
        Like a happy dream:
Like, but not so lasting –
Crocodiles, when fasting,
        Are not all they seem!

Little Birds are choking
        Baronets with bun,
        Taught to fire a gun:
Taught, I say, to splinter
Salmon in the winter –
        Merely for the fun.

Little Birds are hiding
        Crimes in carpet-bags,
        Blessed by happy stags:
Blessed, I say, though beaten –
Since our friends are eaten
        When the memory flags.

Little Birds are tasting
　　Gratitude and gold,
　　Pale with sudden cold
Pale, I say, and wrinkled –
When the bells have tinkled,
　　And the Tale is told.

The Gardener's Song

He thought he saw an Elephant,
    That practised on a fife:
He looked again, and found it was
    A letter from his wife.
'At length I realise,' he said,
    The bitterness of Life!'

He thought he saw a Buffalo
    Upon the chimney-piece:
He looked again, and found it was
    His Sister's Husband's Niece.
'Unless you leave this house,' he said,
    'I'll send for the Police!'

He thought he saw a Rattlesnake
    That questioned him in Greek:
He looked again, and found it was
    The Middle of Next Week.
'The one thing I regret,' he said,
    'Is that it cannot speak!'

He thought he saw a Banker's Clerk
    Descending from the bus:
He looked again, and found it was
    A Hippopotamus:
'If this should stay to dine,' he said,
    'There won't be much for us!'

He thought he saw a Kangaroo
    That worked a coffee-mill:

He looked again, and found it was
    A Vegetable-Pill.
'Were I to swallow this,' he said,
    'I should be very ill!'

He thought he saw a Coach-and-Four
    That stood beside his bed:
He looked again, and found it was
    A Bear without a Head.
'Poor thing,' he said, 'poor silly thing!
    It's waiting to be fed!'

He thought he saw an Albatross
    That fluttered round the lamp:
He looked again, and found it was
    A Penny-Postage Stamp.
'You'd best be getting home,' he said:
    'The nights are very damp!'

He thought he saw a Garden-Door
    That opened with a key:
He looked again, and found it was
    A Double Rule of Three:
'And all its mystery,' he said,
    'Is clear as day to me!'

He thought he saw a Argument
    That proved he was the Pope:
He looked again, and found it was
    A Bar of Mottled Soap.
'A fact so dread,' he faintly said,
    'Extinguishes all hope!'

Disillusionised

I painted her a gushing thing –
　　With years about a score;
I little thought to find them
　　At least a dozen more!

My fancy gave her eyes of blue,
　　A curly auburn head;
I came to find the blue a green,
　　The auburn turned to red!

I painted her a lip and cheek
　　In colour like the rose;
I little thought the selfsame hue
　　Extended to her nose!

I dreamed of rounded features –
　　A smile of ready glee –
But it was not fat I wanted,
　　Nor a grin I hoped to see!

She boxed my ears this morning –
　　They tingled very much –
I own that I could wish her
　　A somewhat lighter touch;

And if you ask me how
　　Her charms might be improved,
I would not have them added to,
　　But just a few removed!

She has the bear's ethereal grace,
    The bland hyaena's laugh –
The footstep of the elephant,
    The neck of a giraffe;

I love her still – believe me –
    Though my heart its passion hides;
She's all my fancy painted her,
    But oh! how much besides!

She's All My Fancy Painted Him

She's all my fancy painted him
    (I make no idle boast);
If he or you had lost a limb,
    Which would have suffered most?

He said that you had been to her,
    And seen me here before;
But, in another character,
    She was the same of yore.

There was not one that spoke to us,
    Of all that thronged the street;
So he sadly got into a 'bus,
    And pattered with his feet.

They sent him word I had not gone
    (We know it to be true);
If she should push the matter on,
    What would become of you?

They gave her one, the gave me two,
    They gave us three or more;
They all returned from him to you,
    Though they were mine before.

If I or she should chance to be
    Involved in this affair,
He trusts to you to set them free,
    Exactly as we were.

It seemed to me that you had been
     (Before she had this fit)
An obstacle, that came between
     Him, and ourselves, and it.

Don't let him know she liked them best,
     For this must ever be
A secret, kept from all the rest,
     Between yourself and me.

The Manlet

In stature the Manlet was dwarfish –
    No burly, big Blunderbore he:
And he wearily gazed on the crawfish
    His Wifelet had dressed for his tea.
'Now reach me, sweet Atom, my gunlet,
    And hurl the old shoelet for luck;
Let me hie to the bank of the runlet,
            And shoot thee a Duck!'

She has reached him his minikin gunlet:
    She has hurled the old shoelet for luck:
She is busily baking a bunlet,
    To welcome him home with his Duck.
On he speeds, never wasting a wordlet,
    Though thoughtlets cling, closely as wax,
To the spot where the beautiful birdlet
            So quietly quacks.

Where the Lobsterlet lurks, and the Crablet
    So slowly and sleepily crawls:
Where the Dolphin's at home, and the Dablet
    Pays long, ceremonious calls:
Where the Grublet is sought by the Froglet:
    Where the Frog is pursued by the Duck:
Where the Ducklet is chased by the Doglet –
            So runs the world's luck!

He has loaded with bullet and powder:
    His footfall is noiseless as air:
But the Voices grow louder and louder,

And bellow, and bluster, and blare.
They bristle before him and after,
        They flutter above and below,
Shrill shriekings of lubberly laughter,
                Weird wailings of woe!

They echo without him, within him:
        They thrill through his whiskers and beard:
Like a teetotum seeming to spin him,
        With sneers never hitherto sneered.
'Avengement,' they cry, 'on our Foelet!
        Let the Manikin weep for our wrongs!
Let us drench him, from toplet to toelet,
                With Nursery-Songs!

'He shall muse upon "Hey! Diddle! Diddle!"
        On the Cow that surmounted the Moon:
He shall rave of the Cat and the Fiddle,
        And the Dish that eloped with the Spoon:
And his soul shall be sad for the Spider,
        When Miss Muffet was sipping her whey,
That so tenderly sat down beside her,
                And scared her away!

'The music of Midsummer-madness
        Shall sting him with many a bite,
Till, in rapture of rollicking sadness,
        He shall groan with a gloomy delight:
He shall swathe him, like mists of the morning,
        In platitudes luscious and limp,
Such as deck, with a deathless adorning,
                The Song of the Shrimp!

'When the Ducklet's dark doom is decided,
        We will trundle him home in a trice:
And the banquet, so plainly provided,
        Shall round into rose-buds and rice:
In a blaze of pragmatic invention
        He shall wrestle with Fate, and shall reign;
But he has not a friend fit to mention,
                So hit him again!'

He has shot it, the delicate darling!
        And the Voices have ceased from their strife:
Not a whisper of sneering or snarling,
        As he carries it home to his wife:
Then, cheerily champing the bunlet
        His spouse was so skilful to bake,
He hies him once more to the runlet,
                To fetch her the Drake!

To Miss Véra Beringer

There was a young lady of station,
'I love man' was her sole exclamation;
But when men cried, 'You flatter,'
She replied, 'Oh! no matter,
Isle of Man is the true explanation.'

Matilda Jane

Matilda Jane, you never look
At any toy or picture-book:
I show you pretty things in vain –
You must be blind, Matilda Jane!

I ask you riddles, tell you tales,
But all our conversation fails:
You never answer me again –
I fear you're dumb, Matilda Jane!

Matilda, darling, when I call,
You never seem to hear at all:
I shout with all my might and main –
But you're so deaf, Matilda Jane!

Matilda Jane, you needn't mind:
For, though you're deaf and dumb and blind,
There's some one loves you, it is plain –
And that is me, Matilda Jane!

Dreams, That Elude the Maker's Frenzied Grasp

Dreams, that elude the Maker's frenzied grasp –
Hands, stark and still, on a dead Mother's breast,
Which nevermore shall render clasp for clasp,
Or deftly soothe a weeping Child to rest –
In suchlike forms me listeth to portray
My Tale, here ended. Thou delicious Fay –
The guardian of a Sprite that lives to tease thee –
Loving in earnest, chiding but in play
The merry mocking Bruno! Who, that sees thee,
Can fail to love thee, Darling, even as I? –
My sweetest Sylvie, we must say 'Good-bye!'

King Fisher Courted Lady Bird

King Fisher courted Lady Bird –
Sing Beans, sing Bones, sing Butterflies!
   'Find me my match,' he said,
   'With such a noble head –
With such a beard, as white as curd –
   With such expressive eyes!'

'Yet pins have heads,' said Lady Bird –
Sing Prunes, sing Prawns, sing Primrose-Hill!
   'And, where you stick them in,
   They stay, and thus a pin
Is very much to be preferred
   To one that's never still!'

'Oysters have beards,' said Lady Bird –
Sing Flies, sing Frogs, sing Fiddle-strings!
   'I love them, for I know
   They never chatter so:
They would not say one single word –
   Not if you crowned them Kings!'

'Needles have Eyes,' said Lady Bird –
Sing Cats, sing Corks, sing Cowslip-tea!
   'And they are sharp – just what
   Your Majesty is not:
So get you gone – 'tis too absurd
   To come a-courting me!'

A Fairy-Duet

'Say, what is the spell, when her fledgelings are cheeping,
     That lures the bird home to her nest?
Or wakes the tired mother, whose infant is weeping,
     To cuddle and croon it to rest;
What's the magic that charms the glad babe in her arms,
     Till it cooes with the voice of the dove?'

''Tis a secret, and so let us whisper it low
And the name of the secret is Love!'

     'For I think it is Love
     For I feel it is Love,
For I'm sure it is nothing but Love!'

'Say, whence is the voice that, when anger is burning,
     Bids the whirl of the tempest to cease?
That stirs the vexed soul with an aching – a yearning
     For the brotherly hand-grip of peace;
Whence the music that fills all our being – that thrills
     Around us, beneath, and above?'

''Tis a secret: none knows how it comes, how it goes
     But the name of the secret is Love!'

     'For I think it is Love,
     For I feel it is Love,
For I'm sure it is nothing but Love!'

'Say whose is the skill that paints valley and hill,
     Like a picture so fair to the sight?

That pecks the green meadow with sunshine and shadow,
    Till the little lambs leap with delight?'

''Tis a secret untold to hearts cruel and cold,
    Though 'tis sung, by the angels above,
In notes that ring clear for the ears that can hear –
    And the name of the secret is Love!'

    'For I think it is Love,
    For I feel it is Love,
For I'm sure it is nothing but Love!'

A Tangled Tale

The elder and the younger knight
They sallied forth at three;
How far they went on level ground
It matters not to me;
What time they reached the foot of hill,
When they began to mount,
Are problems which I hold to be
Of very small account.
The moment that each waved his hat
Upon the topmost peak —
To trivial query such as this
No answer will I seek.
Yet can I tell the distance well
They must have travelled o'er:
On hill and plain, 'twixt three and nine,
The miles were twenty-four.
Four miles an hour their steady pace
Along the level track,
Three when they climbed — but six when they
Came swiftly striding back
Adown the hill; and little skill
It needs, methinks, to show,
Up hill and down together told,
Four miles an hour they go.
For whether long or short the time
Upon the hill they spent,
Two thirds were passed in going up,
One third in the descent.
Two thirds at three, one third at six,
If rightly reckoned o'er,

Will make one whole at four – the tale
Is tangled now no more.

Index of First Lines